NATIONAL INSTITUTE FOR SOCIAL WORK TRAINING SERIES,
NO. 6

NEW DEVELOPMENTS IN CASEWORK

READINGS IN SOCIAL WORK
VOLUME II

NEW DEVELOPMENTS IN CASEWORK

READINGS IN SOCIAL WORK
VOLUME II

COMPILED BY

EILEEN YOUNGHUSBAND
D.B.E., LL.D., J.P.

London

GEORGE ALLEN & UNWIN LTD
RUSKIN HOUSE · MUSEUM STREET

FIRST PUBLISHED IN 1966
SECOND IMPRESSION 1968
FIRST PUBLISHED IN PAPERBACK 1971

SECOND IMPRESSION 1973

© *George Allen & Unwin Ltd, 1966*

ISBN 0 04 361007 2 cased
0 04 361012 9 paper

PRINTED IN GREAT BRITAIN
by W & J Mackay Limited, Chatham

PREFACE

This volume is the second in a series intended to preserve in more permanent form some of the most valuable articles which have appeared in British and American social work journals in the last few years. There are certain articles which are widely used and quoted, which have indeed become standard works but are not always easily available to busy social workers. The aim of this series is thus twofold, both to preserve such articles and make them more widely available, and at the same time by combining together the best that has been written on a given theme by social workers on both sides of the Atlantic to draw attention to recent developments in thought and knowledge.

The present volume includes articles which make use of both psycho-analytic and sociological theory in articulating casework method. It also includes contributions to new thinking about the range and variety of casework techniques with immature and inarticulate clients as well as those who suffer from character disorders.

It is hoped that this series will be widely used by practising social workers, by social teachers and by students not only in Great Britain and the United States but in those many other parts of the world where the profession of social work is advancing towards higher standards of practice.

The National Institute for Social Work Training has received much helpful co-operation from the authors of the articles which form this book and from the journals in which they appeared. In addition to expressing our indebtedness to the authors, the following acknowledgments are made with gratitude to the journals in which the articles originally appeared:

Barnett House, Oxford University, for permission to reproduce 'A New Look at Casework'; *The British Journal of Criminology* (London) for permission to reprint 'Enforcement in Probation Casework'; *The British Journal of Psychiatric Social Work* published by the Association of Psychiatric Social Workers, London, for permission to reprint 'The Function and Use of Relationship between Client and Psychiatric Social Worker', 'Function and Use of Relationship in Psychiatric Social Work' and 'Transference and Reality in the Casework Relationship'; *Case Conference* (London) for permission to reprint 'A Review of Casework Method' and 'Casework Techniques in the Child Care Services'; *Social*

Casework (New York) and the Family Service Association of America, for permission to reprint 'The Generic and Specific in Social Casework Re-examined'; *The Social Service Review* published by the University of Chicago Press, Chicago, for permission to reprint 'The Role Concept and Social Casework: Some Explorations' (Copyright 1961 by the University of Chicago), 'Identity Problems, Role and Casework Treatment' (Copyright 1963 by the University of Chicago), 'Typologies for Caseworkers' (Copyright 1958 by the University of Chicago); *Social Work* (New York), and The National Association of Social Workers for permission to reprint 'Worker-Client Authority Relationships in Social Work'.

CONTENTS

CONTENTS

1

A REVIEW OF CASEWORK METHODS*

MARGARET A. G. BROWN

IN 1915 Mary Richmond, speaking at the American National Conference of Charities and Correction, defined social casework as: 'The art of doing different things for and with different people by co-operating with them to achieve at one and the same time their own and society's betterment.'[1] Although many definitions have been published since 1915 and Mary Richmond herself produced two others, which have perhaps been more frequently quoted, this still seems to express simply and succinctly the essence of casework. Father Swithun Bowers, in his thesis on The Nature of Social Casework, suggested that Mary Richmond's definition was defective as a definition because it could be applied to endeavours beyond the scope of casework.[2] This is true, but here I am concerned less with semantics than with emphasizing again that skill in casework lies in the understanding of the different needs of different people in various social circumstances and in the provision of different, appropriate kinds of help.

Despite the fact that casework was defined in these terms forty-eight years ago and that much has subsequently been written on differential assessment and treatment methods, there is still a good deal of confusion about the nature of casework and the range of caseworkers' activities. For example, in a foreword to a recent publication on casework in the child care service, the following statement occurred: 'True casework occupies only a very small fraction of a child care officer's working hours. It is of course fortunate that this is so, both

---

* Published as a supplement to Case Conference, February 1964 (revised). Based on material collected for an unpublished dissertation 'An Investigation into the Classification of Casework Treatment Activities.' Domanski, Johns and Manly, Smith College, Northampton, Massachusetts, 1960.
[1] Mary Richmond, The Long View. Russell Sage Foundation, New York, 1930, p. 374.
[2] Swithun Bowers, 'The Nature and Definition of Social Casework.' Reprinted from the Journal of Social Casework. Family Service Association of America, 1949, p. 3.

for the officer concerned, and for the authority with a large caseload and too few child care officers. But situations do continually arise when a child care officer must take the initiative and deliberately introduce a casework approach.'[1]

During two refresher courses and a conference for experienced case-workers and student supervisors held during 1962, these comments were made in discussion. 'Casework is only part of the social worker's job. At other times he has to be authoritarian.' 'The caseworker has to do many things that are not pure casework—implementing the law, for instance.' 'We kid ourselves if we think that authority and case-work are compatible.'

In an article entitled 'The Probation Officer as Caseworker' S. R. Eshelby states: 'To-day's probation officer would have no difficulty in defining his work to fit most definitions of casework, for example, (Bowers') "Social casework is an art in which knowledge of the science of human relations and skill in relationship are used to mobilize capacities in the individual, and resources in the community appro-priate for better adjustment between the client and all or any part of his total environment." The probation officer seeks to do just this in his supervisory work, *though he may attempt to do other things as well, such as discipline his client, which may put him outside the fold of case-workers*'[2] (my italics).

Mr Eshelby goes on to discuss some of the difficulties of probation officers in 'applying social casework concepts'. The greatest difficulty he thinks is the probation officer himself. 'I feel fairly confident that part of the attraction of the probation service to men is the apparent opportunity to direct other people's lives. Even if I have deduced the wrong reason it remains true that a number of men officers and some women officers carry out their probation work in an authoritarian, directive way, paying little heed to such things as maintaining a non-judgmental attitude and self determination for the client, and apparently work successfully.

'. . . What is emerging is that there are several types of probation depending upon the personality, attitudes and training of the probation officer. It follows that more careful matching of probation officer and client might be beneficial.

'. . . At present there is no certainty that the highly trained skilled

[1] M. Brooke Willis, Foreword to *Casework in Child Care*, Jean Kastell. Routledge and Kegan Paul, London, 1962, p. ix.
[2] S. R. Eshelby, 'The Probation Officer as Caseworker.' *British Journal of Psychiatric Social Work*, Vol. VI, No. 3, 1962, p. 126.

caseworker is achieving better results than the man or woman who is naturally good with people carrying out simple supportive and directive work.'[1]

There are several points that I would like to comment on here. First, the implication that the use of authority and discipline is not part of casework. This seems to me to be taking too limited a view of casework and of the kinds of relationship which may be helpful to an individual at a particular time. Surely discipline can be a valuable element in casework with certain clients, especially those who feel at the mercy of strong impulses and need help or support in controlling their behaviour, or those who have experienced insecurity and disorder in their lives and temporarily require a firm framework to enable them to function satisfactorily in society. Second, Mr Eshelby suggests that there are different types of probation work, which appear to depend on the personality, attitudes and training of the probation officer, and that in consequence consideration should be given to the matching of officer and probationer. While agreeing with his observations, I would ask whether these different types of casework should not instead depend on the needs of the client, and whether caseworkers in the probation service and elsewhere should not learn to understand better these various needs and to utilize different treatment approaches with different persons. Third, the observation that there is no certainty that the highly trained worker achieves better results than the 'naturally good' worker carrying out simple supportive and directive work: this implies that in the past at least training programmes may not have emphasized sufficiently the variety of methods in casework with the result that students leaving such courses may have tended to place too much reliance on a narrow range of techniques, applying them indiscriminately until experience taught them otherwise.

These points are well brought out in a paper presented by Arthur Hunt at an Association of Psychiatric Social Workers' Refresher Course in 1960, and subsequently published in *Ventures in Professional Co-operation*. He suggests that in approximately 55 per cent of persons under a probation officer's supervision 'cultural, social and heritable' factors are prominent in causation, and he goes on to say 'I do not feel that this type of offender either needs, or could respond to, advanced therapeutic or casework techniques'. He explains that what he means by advanced techniques is: 'A self conscious relationship aimed at revealing transferred residues of past experience which cause perceptual distortion, and its consequences of inappropriate action and manipulation. The use of these necessarily sophisticated techniques has demanded . . . an appreciation of need on the part of the subject and comparative freedom from external pressures of time and conflicting obligation. Such techniques have naturally been most frequently employed in clinical settings. . . .'

Mr Hunt suggests that the bias which appears to exist in training courses is partly due to the fact that a high proportion of casework teachers have matured and developed techniques in settings appropriate to the treatment of the neuroses, as distinct from character disorders or behaviour having a strong cultural determinant, and that 'an impression is created among many students that comparatively inactive techniques are generally applicable in a setting such as probation'. He continues: 'I have finally been forced to the conclusion that whilst practising officers are much alive to the value of insightful and comprehensive casework in certain circumstances (usually those which are analogous to clinical situations), they have found it extraordinarily difficult to apply *advanced casework techniques* generally in the probation setting . . . All too often attempts to apply techniques considered relevant in other settings have been frustrated. . . . I feel that *casework techniques*, with their underlying psychoanalytic origin, are still relevant (in the probation setting) and may be applied usefully and with demonstrable success, even though they may have to be modified until they are barely recognizable'[1] (my italics).

The emphasis here is on the relevance or otherwise, in the probation setting, of a small range of casework techniques directed towards the development of insight in the client. For conceptual convenience Mr Hunt sometimes refers to these techniques as 'advanced', while at other times he and the other authors quoted imply that this group of techniques is synonymous with, or at least representative of casework in general. This is unfortunate, but it does illustrate the tendency during recent years to think of casework in these rather limited terms. Both Mr Hunt and Mr Eshelby make it clear that in their own experience other methods of help are often more useful, and Mr Hunt has now clarified and developed his views in an interesting paper 'Enforcement in Probation Casework', from which two short extracts may be quoted. 'Personal experience of a wide range of delinquents suggests that much antisocial behaviour arises from the failure of a socialization process

[1] A. Hunt, 'The Psychiatric Services and the Social Services: II. Probation.' *Ventures in Professional Co-operation*. Association of Psychiatric Social Workers, London, 1960, pp. 82-4.

and that the compulsive, neurotic, affectionless or seriously unbalanced person is in the minority. Moreover, recognizable in much relatively casual delinquency is the presence of poorly sublimated aggression in which the failure of primary or social institutions of control is in evidence.' ... 'The enforced relationship and casework are not mutually exclusive. Indeed, in many respects the probation casework process is enriched by enforcement, and the explanation appears to centre on the fact that enforcement is an essential component of all early socializing processes.'[1] Caseworkers in all settings have probably intuitively always recognized this and in practice adapted their methods to the differing needs of their clients, but it is helpful, especially for the beginning worker, to have the reasoning spelled out in print.

Casework, as I see it, is a helping activity which is made up of a very large number of constituent activities ranging from the giving of material assistance, through listening, expressing acceptance and re-assurance, suggesting, advising and the setting of limits, to the making of comments that encourage the client to express or suppress his feelings, to examine his situation or to see connections between his present attitudes and behaviour and past experiences. (In a recent study of casework interviews in which I was involved at least sixty-two different activities initiated either by the worker or by the client were identifiable.)[2] These may be utilized and blended in an infinite variety of ways and the caseworker's skill would appear to lie firstly in his ability to understand the needs of his client in relation to the needs of others, and secondly in his ability to relate to his client appropriately, and to employ such methods as will most exactly meet the latter's changing needs. It is hardly necessary to say that this kind of skill is grounded in an extensive knowledge of human beings and society, and an awareness of self which enables the worker to use himself with discrimination in different situations. Since the vast majority of persons referred to social agencies are experiencing stress in some form I would guess that in practice, whatever the setting, most of the techniques employed by caseworkers are supportive in nature and to minimize the value of these by implying that they are not really 'advanced' is to present a misleading picture of casework.

Over the years various attempts have been made to analyse the case-

[1] A. Hunt, 'Enforcement in Probation Casework.' *British Journal of Criminology,* Vol. IV, No. 3, January 1964, pp. 241-51; and in this present book, pp. 206 and 216.

[2] T. P. Domanski, M. M. Johns and M. A. G. Manly, 'An Investigation of a Scheme for the classification of Casework Treatment Activities.' Unpublished thesis. Smith College School for Social Work, Northampton, Mass., 1960.

work process, to look at the numerous small activities of the caseworker during interviews and the reciprocal responses of the client, and to classify these into broad treatment methods. Until some reliable classification is arrived at, it is, of course, impossible to move on to the next stage of studying what kind of approach is successful with different clients experiencing particular kinds of problems and so to eliminate much trial and error. Before reviewing the literature, however, it may be helpful if I define the sense in which the terms 'method' and 'technique' will be used in this article. These words seem to have for many people a cold and calculating connotation, so it should be noted that neither term precludes the warm human concern that is rightly felt to be an essential part of all good social work.

Method is the more comprehensive of the two terms. The Oxford Dictionary definition is 'way of doing something, system of procedure, conscious regularity, orderliness'. I shall use it to include the use of relationship and constituent activities or techniques in casework in a systematic way to achieve certain broad goals. For example, casework can be directed primarily towards supporting the client's ego and helping him to maintain or regain a personal equilibrium and an existing or previous pattern of social adjustment, in which case the method may be described as 'supportive'; or it can be directed towards promoting the client's self understanding with a view to effecting some change in his personality. The method might then be described as 'modifying' or as 'insight development'.

Technique is defined in the Oxford Dictionary as 'manner of artistic execution', 'the part of artistic work that is reducible to formula'. I shall use it to mean the specific response of the caseworker towards the client, such as the giving of money, expressions of interest and sympathy, suggestions, interpretive comments, etc.

In 1921, Virginia Robinson published an 'Analysis of Processes in the Records of Family Case Working Agencies.' She stated: 'It is important to keep clearly in mind from the outset the distinction between those (processes) that have a significance for treatment and those that have only a temporary value—details as to the mechanical process of getting things done which have no real bearing on the development of the case.

'. . . As to the recording of the significant processes . . . there is much difference of opinion. A classification of essential processes which may be made for the convenience of this discussion is: (1) those processes which have to do with altering the material environment in order to meet the client's needs, and (2) those that have to do with the re-education of the client's point of view or habits or attitudes, or the changing of the attitudes of other people toward the client.'[1] This is an early attempt based on observation to distinguish broad methods of casework treatment and to classify these descriptively. No attempt has been made to break down the methods into the component techniques by which re-education or the changing of attitudes is effected.

A slightly more complex analysis of treatment procedures is that described by Mary Richmond in her book *What is Social Casework?* published the following year. She says: 'Before writing this page I tried the experiment of listing each act and policy of each social caseworker responsible, in the six cases cited, for the treatment described. This gave me six long items, many of which were duplicates. By combining these duplicates and trying to classify the items, I found that they fell under the two general heads of "insights" and "acts". Each of these two divided once again—insights to include "an understanding of individuality" and "an understanding of environment"; acts to include "direct action upon the mind" and "indirect action upon the mind". Thus rephrased, my four divisions were:

A. Insight into individuality and personal characteristics.
B. Insight into the resources, dangers and influence of the social environment.
C. Direct action of mind upon mind.
D. Indirect action through the social environment.'[2]

Another early study that is of methodological as well as historical interest is that undertaken by a case committee of the Twin City Chapter of the American Association of Social Workers from 1925 to 1927. Recognizing that interviewing skills constituted an important part of casework treatment, the committee endeavoured to isolate and name the techniques used in ten interviews: two of the interviews were extracts from novels and eight were drawn from the experience of committee members. Altogether eighty-six different techniques were named. It is interesting to observe the extent to which classification appears to be influenced by belief as to what is important in the interviewing process. 'It was found that these techniques grouped themselves into general classifications as follows: (1) the techniques used for lessening tension in the interviewee; (2) techniques used for bringing

---

[1] Virginia Robinson, 'Analysis of Processes in the Records of Family Case Working Agencies.' *The Family*, Vol. III, No. 7, July 1921.
[2] Mary Richmond, *What is Social Casework?* Russell Sage Foundation, New York, 1922, p. 101.

B

or keeping the interviewee to the main issue; (3) techniques used for
helping the interviewee to make difficult admissions; (4) techniques
used for breaking defence mechanisms; (5) techniques used for influencing the judgment of the interviewee; (6) techniques used to help
the interviewer gain time; (7) techniques used to help the interviewer
recover from a bad start. . . . It is evident that our general classifications
are really "processes" and the committee has established, to its satisfaction at least, the conclusion . . . that a process is made up of one or
more techniques.'[1]

In an account of the study, Pearl Salsberry lists the various techniques
that appeared to fall into each of the above mentioned categories. The
first category, for example, was made up of nine different techniques
including 'simulated agreement', 'minimizing the seriousness of the
interviewee's position', 'analysing a general statement into its specific
parts', 'jollying', 'flattery' and 'explaining the agency'. The fourth
category contained eleven techniques, described as follows: 'antici-
pating ultimate outcome', 'abusing for the defence', 'puncture', 'rushing', 'swaying by oratory', 'taking client off his guard', 'using acquired
information', 'putting cards on the table', 'chasing into a corner',
'instilling fear' and 'negation'. A group of techniques which perhaps
has a slightly more positive connotation is the fifth. It includes 'the
transition from known to unknown, reasoning from general to specific
and from specific to general considerations, balancing alternatives, fore-
stalling objections, using interviewee's phraseology, following his leads,
restating the case, preparing for interviewee to state the plan, and yes-
response resulting in clinching the argument.'[2] It is worth noting that
silences were considered to constitute techniques in several processes!

During the decade 1929 to 1939 social workers in Britain and the
United States were largely preoccupied with problems of unemployment and financial insecurity resulting from the economic depression
and, in America at least, with the need to assimilate new knowledge
from the field of psychiatry, and there appears to have been less interest
in examining exactly what went on in casework interviews. The Milford
Conference Report, however, published in 1929, identified 'three fundamental processes' of casework, and it will be observed that specific
mention is made of the process of developing the client's understanding
about himself, as opposed to the worker merely gaining an understanding of the client. 'The goals of social case treatment are both

---

[1] Pearl Salsberry, 'Techniques in Casework.' *The Family*, Vol. IX, No. 7, July 1927,
pp. 154-5.
[2] ibid., p. 156.

ultimate and proximate. The ultimate goal is to develop in the individual the fullest possible capacity for self maintenance in a social group. In attaining both immediate and ultimate goals three fundamental processes interplay at every point: (1) the use by the social caseworker of resources—educational, medical, religious, industrial—all of which have a part in the adjustment of the individual to social living; (2) assisting the client to understand his needs and possibilities; and (3) helping him to develop the ability to work out his own social programme through the use of available resources.

'. . . We could list the "treatment services" given on the statistical cards used by social casework agencies but they would give merely the bare bones of what is involved in social case treatment. The flesh and blood is in the dynamic relationship between social caseworker and the client . . .; the interplay of personalities through which the individual is assisted to desire and achieve the fullest possible development of his personality.'[1] Other attempts to classify casework methods published during the 1930's include those by Burlingham,[2] Lowry,[3] and Hambrecht,[4] in three papers on differential diagnosis and treatment.

An author who has done a good deal of work on this subject and whose analyses of treatment methods are more familiar in this country is Florence Hollis. One of her earliest formulations was published in 1939 in her book *Social Casework in Practice*. She divided treatment processes into 'those aiming to improve the environment in which the person lives and those attempting to increase the client's capacity for meeting whatever environment he finds himself in'. Under the heading 'Reducing environmental pressures' she distinguished direct relief of external pressures by the worker from activity which encourages the client himself to bring about changes in his situation. Under 'Reducing the inner pressures' she identified four main ways in which the caseworker can assist the client to deal adequately with his own reality: (1) by bringing about modification of an inadequate or an over-restrictive conscience; (2) by lessening the need for repression; (3) by reducing feelings of anxiety, inadequacy, and defeat; and (4) by helping

---

[1] *Social Case Work, Generic and Specific. An Outline. A Report of the Milford Conference.* American Association of Social Workers, New York, 1929, p. 29.

[2] Susan Burlingham, 'Differential Diagnosis as a Basis for Selection in a Family Service Agency.' *Diagnostic and Treatment Processes in Family Social Work.* Family Welfare Association of America, New York, 1935, p. 2.

[3] Fern Lowry, 'The Client's Needs as the Basis for Differential Approach in Treatment.' *Differential Approach in Case Work Treatment.* Family Welfare Association of America, New York, 1936, pp. 5-6.

[4] L. M. Hambrecht, 'Psychiatric and Social Treatment: Functions and Correlations.' *Psychiatric Quarterly*, Vol. II, July 1937, pp. 391-423.

the individual to see more clearly the nature of outer reality and his own relationship to it.[1]

Subsequently Miss Hollis revised this classification. In 1949, in *Women in Marital Conflict,* she pointed out that previous treatment classifications had referred sometimes to methods and sometimes to aims and said that her own revised scheme was based on the means (i.e. the processes and techniques) of treatment rather than on its objectives. She outlined four major casework processes:

'*Environmental Modification.* . . . the steps taken by the caseworker to change the environment in the client's favour by the worker's *direct action.*

'*Psychological Support.* . . . Encouraging the client to talk freely and to express his feelings . . .; expressing sympathetic understanding of the client's feelings and acceptance of his behaviour; . . . interest in the client, . . . desire to help; expression of . . . confidence that a way can be found to improve the situation, confidence in the client's ability to solve his difficulty, to make his own decisions; . . . direct encouragement of attitudes that will enable the client to function more realistically as well as more comfortably.

'*Clarification.* . . . Usually accompanies psychological support. . . . The dominant note . . . is understanding by the client of himself, his environment, and/or people with whom he is associated. It is directed towards increasing the ego's ability to see external realities more clearly and to understand the client's own emotions, attitudes and behaviour. . . . The client must be encouraged to talk freely about the situation that is troubling him. . . . Sometimes the caseworker makes direct interpretations concerning the effect or significance of the client's actions or reactions or of those of others with whom he is associated. More often the worker merely asks questions or comments on inconsistencies and inappropriate emotions. Always the effort is to help the client to think more clearly, to react more realistically, and to plan more wisely.

'*Insight.* Insight development involves carrying understanding to a deeper level than that described in clarification. . . . Current and past emotions must be relived in a therapeutic atmosphere in order that some of the affect may be discharged and in order that irrationalities may be brought so clearly to the surface that they can be recognized, at first in the safety of the treatment situation and later in real life.'[2]

---

[1] Florence Hollis, *Social Casework in Practice. Six Case Studies.* Family Welfare Association of America, New York, 1939, pp. 294-9.

[2] Florence Hollis, *Women in Marital Conflict.* Family Service Association of America, New York, 1949, pp. 147-52.

This classification was criticized by Dr Edward Bibring[1] on the grounds that the four concepts were on a different level of abstraction, but it has nevertheless been widely quoted (for example, in *The Probation Service* by Joan King,[2] *A Primer of Social Casework* by Elizabeth Nicholds,[3] and other volumes) and is obviously still being extensively used in courses of professional training. Sometimes, unfortunately, it appears to have been misquoted or quoted out of context, with the result that the inexperienced worker may gain the impression that the ultimate in skilled casework is the use of the fourth method. Florence Hollis herself specifically stated that psychological support was the most useful method with persons facing severe stress; infantile, immature individuals who are essentially in need of guidance; persons suffering from severe neuroses, severe psychosomatic difficulties and mild psychoses. She suggested that insight development could be considered with mildly neurotic persons, but only if the person desired it, could participate in it and benefit from it, and that psychological support was a valuable alternative. She further stated that full and regular psychiatric consultation was *essential* for caseworkers attempting to use insight development. It may be of interest to note that Miss Hollis looked at fifty-one cases, which seemed to have been skilfully handled and in only four of them was this method of insight development used and then along with other methods. She said: 'It is obvious . . . that the emphasis in treatment falls heavily in the area of clarification and psychological support, with environmental support also important and insight development used in only a very few instances.'[4] She also observed that in *the distressingly large number of cases in which clients terminated treatment the caseworker had not created a sufficiently supportive atmosphere.*

Several other classifications of casework treatment methods were published about this time, the one by Lucille Austin contained in her paper 'Trends in Differential Treatment in Social Casework' published in 1948 being particularly comprehensive.[5] She differentiated between two main methods in casework, 'social therapy' and 'psychotherapy', subdividing psychotherapy into 'supportive therapy', 'intermediary or experiential therapy' and 'insight therapy', and analysed each of these in terms of the goals involved and the techniques used.

[1] Edward Bibring, 'Condensation of the Discussion,' *Journal of Social Casework*, Vol. XXX, No. 6, June 1949, p. 258.
[2] Joan S. King (ed.) *The Probation Service,* Butterworth, London, 1958, pp. 69, 75.
[3] Elizabeth Nicholds, *A Primer of Social Casework*, Columbia University Press, New York, 1960, pp. 3-11.
[4] Florence Hollis, *Women in Marital Conflict*, pp. 156-8.
[5] Lucille Austin, 'Trends in Differential Treatment in Social Casework,' *Journal of Social Casework*, Vol. XXIX, No. 6, June 1948, pp. 203-11.

These classifications indicate the extent to which social workers in the United States were making use of the concepts and methods of psychiatry and it therefore seems appropriate to refer to one of the most important of the psychiatric texts published during this period. Dr Franz Alexander in his book *Psychoanalytic Therapy* wrote in 1946: 'We can easily distinguish two general types of psychotherapy—supportive and insight (uncovering) therapy. Supportive therapy is used primarily for the purpose of giving support to the patient's ego with no attempt to effect permanent ego changes; uncovering or insight therapy is used primarily for the purpose of achieving a permanent change in the ego by developing the patient's insight into his difficulties and increasing the ability of his ego to deal with them, through the emotional experiences in the transference situation. Since both types of approach are present in almost all treatments, however, this distinction is not absolute.'[1]

Thomas French, writing in the same volume, also considered that there were two main types of therapeutic approach 'which are employed in endless combination according to the requirements of each particular therapeutic problem', but he named these as 'Manipulation of the Environment' (supportive therapy is included in this category) and 'Modification of Behaviour Patterns'.[2] In 1953 and 1958 the Family Service Association of America and the Community Service Society of New York published somewhat similar analyses of casework.[3, 4]

Meanwhile Florence Hollis in a paper presented in Boston in 1955 indicated that she had revised her earlier fourfold classification and said that she had come to the conclusion that there were really only two major forms of casework treatment—'supportive treatment' and 'development of self awareness'. Both forms of treatment had the aim of improving the individual's functioning, but supportive treatment attempted this without substantial increase in self understanding, whereas the latter aimed to increase the individual's awareness of previously hidden aspects of his feelings and behaviour. She wrote: 'The most important distinction between the two forms of treatment lies in whether or not an attempt is made to bring suppressed material into consciousness, for as soon as we move in the direction of uncovering

---

[1] Franz Alexander and Thomas French, *Psychoanalytic Therapy*, Ronald Press Co., New York, 1946, p. 102.
[2] ibid., pp. 132-40.
[3] Family Service Association of America, *Scope and Methods of the Family Service Agency*, New York, 1953.
[4] Community Service Society of New York, *Method and Process in Social Casework*, Family Service Association of America, New York, 1958.

A REVIEW OF CASEWORK METHODS

hidden material we move in the direction of arousing anxiety.'[1] In a more recent article Miss Hollis elaborated on this very important theme. She pointed out that development of self awareness, involving clarification and investigation of suppressed or uncomprehended material, makes great demands on the client's ego for several reasons. First because in order to encourage self examination the worker has to refrain from making reassuring comments at points where they could be made. This may mean that temporarily the client's discomfort is increased. Secondly, feelings of anger towards the worker as the source of the discomfort may be aroused in the client. Thirdly, if the client is able to think about material that has been suppressed or is consciously painful, there will inevitably be a period of increased anxiety until he has come to terms with it. Fourthly, the very business of becoming aware of and laying aside certain defences means that he is more exposed and therefore more vulnerable to pain and discomfort.

She continued: 'For these reasons it is essential that when [development of self-awareness] is undertaken the worker be certain that the client has the kind of ego that can sustain itself during a period of tension without recourse to too much regression, extensive additional symptom formations, unwise acting out, or immobilization.

'Furthermore, one must be sure that the techniques used in bringing suppressed ideas to the surface do not unloose more buried material than the caseworker knows how to deal with. The individual in other words must be one with a healthy capacity to both repress and suppress painful material. Otherwise both worker and client will be overwhelmed by the mental content that is unleashed when suppressed material is invited to full consciousness. This is a point particularly to be kept in mind, for it is a great temptation when people talk easily about their life experiences and feelings to think that they would be admirable candidates for this kind of help, when in actuality the very opposite may be true. Some psychotics talk very easily about things which less sick people would keep deeply buried in the unconscious.

'Clarification and the pursuit of causative understanding of the self must be used sparingly. In actuality only a small proportion of our work is predominantly of this type. With many clients it should not be used at all. With many it is not needed. It should be a major tool of treatment only when the client's personality organization is relatively sound or where a circumscribed area which brings relief with a minimum of anxiety can be clarified, where the nature of the psychosocial

---

[1] Florence Hollis, 'Personality Diagnosis in Casework,' *Ego Psychology and Dynamic Casework*, ed.H. Par ad, Family Service Association of America, New York, 1958, p. 86.

dysfunctioning makes it appropriate, where motivation toward self-understanding can be developed, and where there are appropriate safeguards in terms of the worker's skill and the availability of psychoanalytic consultation. . . . In general the milder forms of symptom neurosis and neurotic character. When such procedures are used with other types of personality patterns it should be with caution and with particular attention to the client's anxiety and the handling of it.'[1]

Miss Hollis's latest work *Casework—A Psychosocial Therapy* deals exhaustively with these and many other aspects of casework treatment. It is the most comprehensive and ambitious book yet to have appeared on the subject and will be referred to again, when the present theoretical position is considered. In the meantime, two case illustrations may help to bring home the particular points discussed above.

In the first case a social worker tried to assist an adolescent youth towards the development of self awareness, in the sincere belief that if the boy could gain insight into the connection between his barely suppressed aggressive feelings against authority and the poor relationship which he had experienced with his father, he would be better able to deal with them. All the evidence showed that, far from being 'mildly neurotic', the boy was a very immature individual with poorly developed defences against anxiety and precarious controls over his behaviour. In interview, however, the worker ignored the lad's unresponsiveness to his questioning, and in between long periods of silence probed steadily away. Every defence put up by the boy was 'seen through' and interpreted despite the latter's increasing tension. Finally, after three-quarters of an hour, the boy was dismissed with the injunction that he 'should think further about his feelings'. The worker was surprised and saddened when his client smashed the office window on the way out and careered down the street kicking at parked cars and splintering most of the milk bottles in sight.

The second case is that of Mrs T, a 31-year-old married woman who applied for help to a psychiatric out-patient clinic. At the time she was hallucinating and suffering from numerous phobias and obsessive compulsive symptoms to the extent that she was almost incapacitated. She was afraid of being alone, going out, answering the telephone, going upstairs, and was preoccupied with thoughts of death, accidents and suicide. A detailed history was obtained, which revealed that she had had an extremely disturbed background. At the intake case committee

---

[1] Florence Hollis, 'Analysis of Casework Treatment Methods and their Relationship to Personality Change,' *Smith College Studies in Social Work*, Vol. XXXII, No. 2, February 1962, pp. 113-14.

it was felt that the severity of her symptoms contra-indicated any attempt at insight therapy, and the psychiatric registrar (in his second year of post-graduate training) to whom she was assigned for treatment, was advised to use a supportive approach. From the outset, however, the psychiatrist made extensive use of uncovering and insight directed techniques. At various times he interpreted her defences, encouraged the expression of hostile feelings, and there was much discussion of sexual problems which she clearly found very disturbing. She began to be silent in interviews, then to miss appointments, and finally withdrew from treatment altogether. She stated that she felt she was not getting anywhere and felt too uncomfortable during interviews to continue.

The following year Mrs T again approached the clinic for help. She was in a state of panic and gave the impression of being a very sick woman. Once more her application was considered by the case committee and again supportive therapy was recommended. This time she was assigned to a caseworker. During the first interview she talked disjointedly and at great length, expressing extreme aggression towards her small son who she was afraid was becoming homosexual, intense fear and hatred of her mother and father, and a sense of profound unworthiness. She felt hopeless about her marriage and began to describe incidents in her very early childhood which she knew had given rise to her present fears and also recalled dreams which had upset her. The caseworker wavered between permissively listening to this outpouring of feelings, implicitly encouraging their expression by 'going along' with Mrs T's recollections of traumatic events in her early childhood, and offering active support and reassurance. During the next two or three interviews this pattern continued and gradually the caseworker, like the first therapist, was drawn into making occasional interpretive comments, with the result that Mrs T became increasingly ambivalent about continuing treatment. In reviewing the course of interviews in some detail it became clear that, following the use of exploratory and interpretive techniques, Mrs T would become resistant and disturbed, but better integrated after support had been given.

The caseworker wrote in an interim summary: 'About Christmas time she appeared torn between her wish to continue seeing me and to experience a corrective emotional relationship that was in many respects helpful to her, and what I now think to be her need to protect herself from my techniques. Following the holiday she "forgot" an appointment, and it was then that I decided to use consistently supportive techniques, no matter how many opportunities she provided for discussion of her underlying problems. During the subsequent two months of supportive casework she has made good progress. Her relationship with her husband and children has improved, her appearance has altered for the better and she has shown many signs of increased ego integration. As her dependency needs have been more adequately met at home, so she has become less dependent on interviews and these have now been reduced in frequency.'

The closing summary, written three months later, went as follows: 'During the final three months of treatment progress has been maintained; Mrs T's pseudo-neurotic symptoms have almost entirely disappeared and she is now able to lead a fairly normal life. My techniques have continued to be primarily supportive and discussion of her problems has been indirect, for example in the context of her children's development, films she has seen and so on. As her anxiety has lessened and as her symptoms have been replaced by more healthy defence mechanisms, she has been able to move on to a constructive consideration of her basic problems, to gain some insight into the origin of these and to put her increased understanding into practice in the form of modified behaviour and attitudes towards her family. Mrs T has expressed much satisfaction in her improved condition and ability to function in the roles expected of her. She recognizes that she has not resolved all her problems, but feels realistically that she is able to manage independently for the time being.'

These cases are, of course, extreme examples, but they serve to underline the point that as caseworkers we must know what we are doing. As Miss Hollis has reminded us, our methods must always be evaluated in relation to 'the nature of the problem, the client's motivation and the capacity of his ego to deal constructively with anxiety'.[1] Most of us, I think, instinctively employ supportive methods with the vast majority of persons who come for help in difficulty; nevertheless there does appear to be some tendency, particularly amongst partially trained or inexperienced workers, to regard these methods as something less than 'real casework' and to attempt to use an approach that may not be merely inappropriate, but in certain cases actually harmful. In a psychiatric setting, for instance, a patient can usually protect himself from techniques that arouse too much anxiety by failing to keep appointments. The probationer, however, is not in this happy position. If he neglects to report he commits a breach of his probation order. It is extremely important, therefore, that all caseworkers acquire skill, through training and experience, in establishing different types of

[1] ibid., p. 117.

relationships with different individuals and in utilizing a wide range of treatment techniques appropriate to the needs of each. As Charlotte Towle said in 1946, some clients become confused, anxious and frustrated in a neutral casework relationship and it is then advisable 'to be supportive, that is to use authority, meet dependency, impose demands and convey moral judgements in a sustaining way, so that the individual may become more self-determining or, at least, less self destructive in his behaviour.'[1]

At the present time many new social work training courses are being established in this country and it behoves those who are concerned with casework teaching to pay particular attention to the differential aspects of casework. Otto Pollak pointed out in a recent article that the principles of casework appropriate for treatment of neurotic clients have by and large been generalized in the sub-culture of the profession, so that problems arise when social workers are confronted with, for example, persons suffering from character disorder. He postulated that if most caseworkers have a neurotic type of personality, then it would be within their own experience that the treatment process is liberating rather than binding.[2] There is a good deal of evidence to support the hypothesis that workers do tend to use with their clients those methods that they may personally find or have found to be helpful. It has, for instance, often been observed that casework students and psychiatrists in training, as they gain insight into their own personalities, frequently attempt to use interpretive techniques with their patients or clients. When the response to these is unfavourable, the student may complain to his supervisor that he has not been assigned a suitable client (patient) or that he is unable to do 'real' casework (psychotherapy). It may take a year or more before he begins to appreciate that the majority of his clients may require help of a supportive nature only and that supportive techniques can and do bring about changes in attitudes and behaviour.

In some of the group experiments that are now being undertaken in this country there is a similar need to make sure that methods that have been used successfully to develop self knowledge in caseworkers are not employed indiscriminately with groups of acting-out adolescent delinquents. Careful selection of group members and the adaptation of techniques to their needs must be undertaken if we are to avoid many mistakes in group therapy.

I should like to turn now to one of the fundamental issues facing the

---

[1] Charlotte Towle, 'Social Casework in Modern Society,' *Social Service Review*, Vol. XX, No. 2, June 1946, pp. 165-79.

[2] Otto Pollak, 'The Treatment of Character Disorders—A Dilemma in Casework Culture,' *Social Service Review*, Vol. XXXV, No. 2, June 1963, pp. 128-31.

caseworker, namely how to help a person overcome the difficulties which are affecting his life in society. The point has been made that the skill of helping lies not only in the careful assessment of the individual and his situation, but also in the differential use of the professional relationship and associated casework techniques. No matter how experienced we are we all need to review frequently our own practice and to ask ourselves what our particular tendency is in casework. Do we adopt a rather stereotyped approach with everyone—anxious mother, delinquent youth, ambulatory schizophrenic alike—or do we vary in the relationships we establish? Are we always permissive and accepting, or (benevolently) authoritarian? Do we habitually listen passively, encourage the expression of feelings, explore our clients' early backgrounds; or is our tendency to take an active part in interviews, offering advice and suggestions, and setting limits? It is so much easier to observe the characteristic approaches of our colleagues in casework than to know our own. If we think that we do tend to react similarly to different clients, is this because it is 'us', because we believe this to be the correct casework approach, or because it really seems to work best in all cases? If we vary our methods, what is our rationale? Do we respond intuitively 'playing it by ear', or have we some ideas born of our own and other peoples' experience about the kinds of methods that are successful with different kinds of individuals that enable us to meet appropriately their differing needs?

The development of casework in the United States makes fascinating reading. We are told of marked pendulum swings from overactivity and directiveness to excessive passivity and drifting, from over-intellectualized analysis of cause and effect relationships to unscientific wallowing in feelings and belittling of intellectual knowledge, from indiscriminate use of social resources to exclusive exploration of emotional factors.[1] Yet at the same time, from the literature reviewed above, we see how during the inter-war period particularly the differential methods of casework were being worked out. The techniques developed by Freud, which so influenced American casework in the 1930's, arose chiefly from his experience in the analysis of neurotic disorders—disorders which appear, in retrospect, to have been related in part to the prevailing social system. Nowadays, as Otto Pollak has pointed out, our society seems to support the development of character disorders. 'Id gratifications are prominently offered in overt and hidden form, while the waning power of generally accepted morality leaves the super-

[1] Annette Garrett, 'Historical Survey of the Evolution of Casework,' *Journal of Social Casework*, Vol. XXX, No. 6, June 1949, p. 223.

ego forces unsupported.' No longer can caseworkers rely solely on the liberating techniques that were so useful (in America) in pre-war years in helping persons to free themselves of sexual and aggressive inhibitions. We must now turn our attention to developing methods that are equally useful with individuals who have too much feeling flowing into action, too little sense of guilt, too few inhibitions—methods that lead to the development of a sense of social responsibility in the client without being a cover for counter-transference reactions;[1] in other words a more skilful, conscious use of the good parent type of relationship that has long been used by caseworkers and found to be effective.

Within recent years certain caseworkers in this country too have been working out for themselves the principles of differential treatment. Elizabeth Irvine in a paper on 'Research into Problem Families', published in 1954, drew attention to the extreme immaturity of many parents of such families and outlined the methods of help which seemed to have proved most effective. For example she wrote: 'The worker has most chance of success if he plays the part of a warm, permissive and supportive parent, thus supplying the basic experiences of the early stage of socialization, which for some reason the client seems to have missed. With great patience and tact, the client can sometimes be led through a phase corresponding to that in which the child likes to "do it with mother" to one in which he begins to taste the satisfaction of "doing it myself".'[2]

Dr T. A. Ratcliffe expressed similar views in 1957,[3] and both these authors subsequently published valuable papers on the differential use of relationship which should be read in full.[4, 5] For the purpose of this article, however, an extract from Dr Ratcliffe's later paper is given as it is especially relevant. 'The most important criterion of assessment (for relationship therapy) is the level of emotional and social maturity of the client . . . in terms of capacity for and experience of relationships. . . . There are many clients whose early experience of relationships was so unsatisfactory that they were never wholly able to work through the

---

[1] Pollak, loc. cit., p. 127.
[2] Elizabeth E. Irvine, 'Research into Problem Families: Theoretical Questions arising from Dr. Blacker's Investigation,' *British Journal of Psychiatric Social Work*, No. 9, May 1954, p. 27.
[3] T. A. Ratcliffe, 'Personality Factors,' *The Problem Family*, Institute for the Study and Treatment of Delinquency, London, 1958.
[4] Elizabeth E. Irvine, 'Transference and Reality in the Casework Relationship,' *British Journal of Psychiatric Social Work*, Vol. III, No. 4, 1956. Republished in *Relationship in Casework*, Association of Psychiatric Social Workers, London, 1964, pp. 53-66; and in this present book, pp. 108-123.
[5] T. A. Ratcliffe, 'Relationship Therapy and Casework,' *British Journal of Psychiatric Social Work*, Vol. V, No. 1, 1959.

initial experience of relationships within the family, the "give and take" of such contacts, the feeling of being approved of, the capacity to internalize controls and standards, and so on. In brief they have failed to mature in this respect. They feel inadequate, and unsure of their contacts; they still see situations narcissistically; they react badly and often impulsively to frustration and criticism. Such people need a parental relationship through which they can experience the relationship patterns they have not had; and thus a parental relationship appropriate to the "maturity level" which the client has reached. This assessment of maturity level, and of the role needed in the relationship, is often a technically difficult task; and it may require a number of interviews to complete.'[1]

In general authors on both sides of the Atlantic have approached the subject from a developmental point of view and have laid stress on the importance of a thorough understanding of the stage of emotional maturity reached by the individual and on the use of an appropriate relationship and techniques. Reiner and Kaufman[2] give a most useful exposition of the use of a 'nurturing' relationship with immature persons suffering from character disorders, while Ferard and Hunnybun[3] describe in the main methods of casework more suited to those with neurotic disorders. Michael Power in his review of Ferard and Hunnybun's book *The Caseworker's Use of Relationships* writes: 'Maybe it is because this book describes so well certain kinds of casework that it becomes clearer that there are other kinds, all equally informed and guided by the same theoretical principles based upon psychoanalytic theory, but different in their techniques and application of the theory. That described in this book may be best used to help people whose ego is reasonably well developed and who have a fairly clear sense of identity, but who are beset with problems, the solution of which seems elusively beyond their grasp and who need additional insight before they are able to attain sufficient control over their own feelings and their environment. Different would be the immature people who need the experience of a relationship in which they can grow and gradually and painfully attain some degree of psychological maturity before they can be expected to carry the responsibilities of adults.'[4]

Several authors draw a distinction between those individuals who,

[1] ibid., p. 4.
[2] B. S. Reiner and I. Kaufman, *Character Disorders in Parents of Delinquents*, Family Service Association of America, New York, 1959.
[3] M. L. Ferard and N. K. Hunnybun, *The Caseworker's Use of Relationships*, Tavistock Publications, London, 1962.
[4] Michael Power, 'Varieties of Casework' (Review article), *Social Work*, Vol. XIX, No. 4, October 1962.

whatever their chronological age, are still emotionally at an infantile stage of development and therefore need 'primary' emotional experiences of love, care, shelter, control and guidance, and those who have to some extent matured beyond infancy, but whose unsatisfactory experiences have given rise to conflicts, defences and inhibitions which cause problems in living, and who need corrective 'secondary' experiences.[1] (In psychoanalytic terms, the distinction is between the pre-oedipal and post-oedipal stages of development; in clinical terms it is between the psychopathic personality, character disorders, and the neuroses.) This developmental approach to the client provides a valuable guide to treatment. From our observation of his present mode of functioning, it is possible to deduce with a fair amount of accuracy the nature of his past experiences, the chief sources of anxiety, the adequacy of the defences against this and the stage of maturity that he has reached. For instance, the individual who has difficulty in establishing satisfactory relationships, who is excessively demanding, who lives solely in the present and cannot postpone immediate satisfactions for the sake of long term gains, and who has a very inaccurate perception of reality, has probably experienced insecurity in childhood and is likely to need the support of a casework relationship which provides consistent love, care, firmness, and frustration when necessary, a relationship which gradually and continuously adapts as he becomes capable of greater independence and acquires a better understanding of the outside world and capacity to satisfy his needs in socially acceptable ways. In contrast the relatively adequate, well integrated person who is able to function successfully in many areas of his life, who comes for help with some neurotic problem affecting his relationships, may come from a comparatively stable, perhaps rather inhibiting background. His need may well be for a permissive relationship. Always the caseworker's aim should be to understand the basic source of anxiety and to alleviate it in some measure through the provision of new, satisfying and maturing experiences.

The Association of Psychiatric Social Workers put it thus: 'The casework relationship is not the same for every client, but should, as far as possible, be adjusted to meet the varying need of different clients. One important function of the casework relationship is to supply in some measure those experiences necessary for satisfactory emotional development, which have been lacking in the life of the individual

---

[1] See for example: B. E. Dockar-Drysdale, 'The Outsider and the Insider in a Therapeutic School,' *Ventures in Professional Co-operation*, Association of Psychiatric Social Workers, London, 1960, pp. 13-14.

client. Thus an inhibited and submissive client may need to be encouraged to speak his mind to the worker, and to express his feelings of criticism and dissatisfaction as a prelude to developing the ability to stand up for himself in other situations. On the other hand, a client whose pattern of behaviour is to control and exploit people until they eventually throw him over, may need to have a relationship with someone who resists all attempts to manipulate him, while remaining friendly and sympathetic. Thus the balance between firmness and permissiveness has to be finely adjusted to the needs of the client, and should not be influenced by the worker's own need, for example, to control situations himself, or to keep on the right side of everybody.'[1]

An experienced worker with advanced training recently said in the course of a case discussion, that he felt that he did not have 'sufficient ammunition to knock a hole in (the client's) wall of defences'. This and similar remarks which are made all too frequently suggests that (in this country at least) too little attention has been paid in casework courses to the constructive functions of defences and the need often to conserve and support these in casework.

Anna Freud in *The Ego and the Mechanisms of Defence* postulated that the individual develops defences against anxiety (i.e. a state of tension which it is beyond the person's capacity to master) arising from three sources—the super-ego, objective reality, and the instincts. Super-ego anxiety is the easiest to relieve. As the individual develops a relationship with a worker who is accepting and non-condemning his sense of guilt and the unconscious conflict decreases, and he becomes able to permit cautious expression of instinctual urges and feelings. Clients suffering from super-ego anxiety sometimes find their way to a probation office—their offence may have arisen from a wish for punishment, but more often they will be seen in psychiatric clinics and consulting rooms, in marriage guidance offices and in child guidance clinics. The permissive interviewing techniques which have been developed in these settings are usually most helpful to them.

Individuals suffering from 'objective anxiety' (i.e. that arising from external circumstances) are well known in most social work agencies. Problems of food, accommodation, money, work, adverse. family relationships, and so on are the special province of the caseworker. Techniques, such as material help, sympathy, interest, advice, discussion, clarification, are often of greatest help here.

The third type of anxiety, 'instinctual anxiety', is considered by

[1] Association of Psychiatric Social Workers, *The Essentials of Social Casework*, London, 1963, p. 2.

Anna Freud to be the most difficult to alleviate, particularly in an analytic situation. She writes: 'The only pathological states which fail to react favourably to analysis are those based on a defence prompted by the patient's dread of the strength of his instincts. In such a case there is a danger that we may annul the defensive measures of the ego without being able immediately to come to its assistance. . . . This most deadly struggle of the ego to prevent itself from being submerged by the id . . . is essentially a matter of quantitative relations. All that the ego asks for in such a conflict is to be reinforced. . . . In so far as analysis can strengthen it by bringing the unconscious id-contents into consciousness, it has a therapeutic effect. . . . But, in so far as the bringing of the unconscious activities of the ego into consciousness has the effect of disclosing the defensive processes and rendering them inoperative, the *result of the analysis is to weaken the ego still further and to advance the pathological process*[1] (author's italics).

It is with persons beset by instinctual anxiety that caseworkers seem to be increasingly concerned. The suggestion that our present society in its swing away from Victorian morality has tended to ally itself with the id forces has important implications for social work. Free expression of instinctual drives in direct form is incompatible with civilization and some social workers, particularly those employed in penal settings, are entrusted among other things with the important function of helping those who have poor control over their urges to develop greater capacity to endure frustration. Techniques which relieve anxiety and strengthen precarious defences, such as consistent acceptance, limit setting, reassurance and understanding discussion within the context of a positive relationship are most likely to be of assistance here. In an article on 'Casework and Agency Function', Clare Winnicott rightly pointed out that in probation, for example, the delinquent may be: 'unconsciously looking for a human being to become a respected and controlling authority, because this is just what he has been deprived of in his family relationships. . . . The probation officer can humanize the machinery of the law but he cannot side-step it without missing the whole point of the symptom and the needs of the client. If he does miss the point, the client either gives up hope or commits another offence to ensure the re-instatement of legal machinery.'[2]

J. St John quotes a probationer who complains that his probation officer had not been strict enough: 'If he'd given me a good telling off,

[1] Anna Freud, *The Ego and the Mechanisms of Defence*, Hogarth Press, London, 1954, pp. 69-70.
[2] Clare Winnicott, 'Casework and Agency Function,' *Case Conference*, Vol. VIII, No. 7, January 1962, p. 181-2.

C

it might have been different. I'd have pulled myself together like. Even when I'd been up for a breach he still gave me the old syrup. After that probation seemed a farce.'[1]

In casework with psychotic or near-psychotic patients the psychiatric social worker has a similar responsibility to support and strengthen that part of the patient's personality which is in touch with reality and which may be threatened by an eruption of instinctual impulses, and this means the ego, including its defensive operations. Mrs T, the patient referred to earlier, is an example of a borderline psychotic who needed much ego support. Attempts to increase her genetic understanding of her difficulties merely led to an increase in anxiety amounting to panic. Only after she had succeeded in re-establishing necessary defences was she able gradually to start working things out for herself and to begin to perceive how her present irrational fears were related to her past experiences.

Sufficient has been said to indicate that caseworkers need to apply themselves with renewed thought to 'the art of doing different things for and with different people'.[2] The point has been made that skill in casework does not lie only in the use of a small range of techniques directed towards the development of self-knowledge, although this does demand skill of a kind, but in the careful assessment of the social situation, personality structure, stage of development and sources of anxiety of each individual, and then in the sensitive, flexible, discriminating use of appropriate methods of help. Depending on the changing needs of the client at any particular time, we may be warm or detached, active or passive, directive or permissive, verbal or silent, moralistic or non-judgmental in our approach. As Florence Hollis points out in her latest book: 'The treatment of any person is an individualized blend of procedures, themes, and goals. The nature of the blend is not a matter of individual worker artistry or intuition, important though these may be. On the contrary, choice and emphasis follow definite principles and rest upon most careful evaluation of the nature of the client's problem, external and internal causative factors and their modifiability, the client's motivation, and pertinent aspects of his personality. In addition, there must be comprehension of the nature, effects, and demands of the different types of casework procedures and of the criteria by which the worker can match the client's needs and capacities with the particular combination of procedures most likely to be of value in enabling him to overcome, or at least lessen, his difficulties. . . . The evaluative

---

[1] J. St. John, *Probation—The Second Chance*, Vista Books, London, 1961, p. 34.
[2] M. Richmond, *The Long View*, loc. cit.

process is an ongoing one, with the emphasis in treatment varying in harmony with the changing needs and capacities of the client.'[1] That a careful blending of techniques is necessary in almost all cases is now fairly widely recognized in the literature.

The following short interview illustrates well the skilful, even if intuitive, use of a variety of casework techniques. It demonstrates an unselfconscious ability to communicate with and to adapt to the swiftly changing needs of a person in distress, and repays careful study.

Sandra is a 16-year-old girl from an extremely disturbed background who spent four years at a school for maladjusted children, but who had eventually to leave because of her difficult behaviour. Turned out of home by her mother, she had problems over work and accommodation, and committed offences for which she was placed on probation. Then began a long period of shelter and hostel life with many changes of residence, Sandra making more and more demands on her probation officer.

The previous day Sandra had attempted to 'phone me, but I was not available. She then visited the clinic and had a scene with the psychiatrist and refused to return. Her outburst at the clinic was mainly directed towards me.

To-day she called and went as usual straight to the waiting room. I was unaware that she was there and was engaged on the 'phone. Suddenly there was a frenzied knocking on the door and a furious face looked round and demanded, 'How much longer have I to wait?' I replied, 'I am engaged on the 'phone—would you please sit in the waiting room?' She was furious. When free, I invited her in and she said, 'May I telephone Miss L at the YWCA? It is important.' I said, 'Yes' and in an arrogant manner she went to the 'phone, but the line was engaged. She tried again and again and then threw down the telephone, using some extremely foul language. I said, 'Sandra, would you please not use this language?' For fully two minutes her jaw trembled and with difficulty she held back the tears. She then turned and said, 'You don't understand me, only Miss L does.' I replied, 'You are missing Miss L quite a bit, aren't you?' She did not reply.

The atmosphere was still very tense and she then walked over to a drawer in which I keep quite a number of personal things, including some small boxes with jewellery. (Christmas gifts from probationers.) Like a child she went through each of the boxes and played around for quarter of an hour in this way. She then got up and went to the mirror in my room, and started to pin up her hair. During this time I said nothing. She suddenly turned and said, 'So this means that when my

[1] Florence Hollis, Casework—A Psychological Therapy, Random House, New York, 1964, p. 243.

probation is over I shall not be able to come here.' I replied, 'You know you will always have a place here. After all, haven't you been treating me as your mother over the past few months?' She answered with a smile on her face, 'My mother doesn't nag like you.' I then said, 'And what have I been nagging about?' to which she replied, 'Work and how I hate it. If only I could marry a wealthy man.' I said, 'Even a wealthy man would not want to see his wife lying in bed all day. No marriage can last in that way.'

We then went on to discuss her inability to get up in the morning and her depression, but she tired of this, or did not want to discuss it, and began to yawn. I began to put my papers away and asked her if she would like to accompany me along the street to the station. Before leaving the office she made a circle round a date on the calendar and said, 'This is my birthday.'

We walked along the street looking at a number of shops. It was a pleasant evening and she now seemed fairly happy. Suddenly and quite naturally she took my arm. At the station I purchased her ticket to the hostel and my own ticket home and said goodbye.

This article has been an attempt to summarize some of the thinking that has gone on during the past forty years about the methods of social casework and the principles which seem to be emerging concerning their differential application. (For example the principle identified by Miss Hollis that 'the more fully and deeply the worker encourages the client to know himself the more caution is needed in making certain that the client's ego is able to deal constructively with the anxiety likely to be aroused'.[1]) The value of supportive methods of help has deliberately been stressed because so much of the casework literature published in this country during the 1950-60 decade focusses on the interpretive type of work appropriate for relatively mature and well integrated individuals, and students and others seemed to be gaining the impression that this was the method *par excellence* to use with all clients. Studies such as that undertaken by Noel Timms[2] of what in fact social workers actually do in interviews are of course a most useful corrective to such impressions, but as yet few have been attempted in Britain.

It may be debated whether in the final analysis different methods and techniques have any real significance in casework. Elizabeth Irvine in 1956 emphasized the importance of the caseworker's attitude and commented on the fact that different workers obtain satisfactory results with

---

[1] Hollis, 'Analysis of Casework Treatment Methods and Their Relationship to Personality Change,' loc. cit., p. 115.

[2] Noel Timms, *Psychiatric Social Work in Great Britain (1929-1962)*, Routledge and Kegan Paul, London, 1964, pp. 105-8.

a variety of techniques, and that any given technique could prove unsuccessful if counter-transference becomes predominantly negative.[1] Paul Halmos in a more recent article reminded us of the central place of love in various forms of psychotherapy, and questioned whether the expression of this love could be accurately described as a skill, which could be techically mastered and used deliberately.[2] I am sure that most of us would agree with both these writers that the worker's positive attitude of love and concern for the client is of far greater importance than the means by which it is expressed. But surely the mode of expression is also important. The issue is not 'Love or Skill?' (to quote the title of Dr Halmos' paper) but love and skill. If casework is to be of help to the many different persons facing various problems who come to social work agencies, both these elements are essential. Love is of basic significance even when it is clumsily expressed. How much better in a professional service that it should be allied to knowledge and skill and expressed in ways most suited to the client's needs.

As caseworkers we try to communicate with a wide range of individuals in many different situations, to understand their anxieties and the manner in which these are concealed or expressed and to offer appropriate help in a form most acceptable to them. We may be required to perform some short-term material service; we may have to provide the long-term 'nurturing relationship' described by Kaufman and others[3] in which an emotionally deprived, infantile individual experiences closeness and trust, identifying with the caseworker before becoming able to function more successfully and independently—the type of casework that has been developed by Family Service Units; or perhaps with a mildly hysterical client, the need may be for a more reflective, detached approach. Such flexibility and discernment in helping does not come naturally to most of us and it is therefore important that we should be cognizant of the various methods of casework that have been identified and develop skill in using them to greatest effect.

---

[1] Irvine, 'Transference and Reality in the Casework Relationship,' loc. cit., p. 62; and in this present book, pp. 108-123.
[2] Paul Halmos, 'Love or Skill?' New Society, Vol. III, No. 77, March 19, 1964.
[3] Irving Kaufman, 'Differential Methods in Treating Persons with Character Disorders,' Smith College Studies in Social Work, Vol. XXXII, No. 3, 1962.

2

A NEW LOOK AT CASEWORK*

ELIZABETH E. IRVINE

CASEWORK as a method of personal help has never resolved its identity crisis. It emerged laboriously from a primary preoccupation with the material predicaments of clients and their moral character, thanks to a growing knowledge of psycho-analytic theory and technique. It then underwent a phase of identification with this very potent parent-figure, during which there was a tendency to define itself with reference to psycho-analysis or psycho-therapy of an analytic kind, and in very similar terms. Such a definition of 'advanced casework techniques' is given by Arthur Hunt,[1] who adds, however, that in his experience these much valued methods do not correspond with the needs of many clients of such services as probation, who need a simpler, and sometimes a more directive, approach. Margaret Brown[2] emphasizes the need for a broad range of techniques, applied with sensitive discrimination according to the needs of the client. Since I must acknowledge some share of responsibility for the tendency to equate casework skill with the narrow range of techniques described by Hunt as 'advanced', it may be appropriate to record a change of heart.

To arrive at an understanding of what advanced casework is, we have to ask ourselves two questions:

(a) What is casework?

(b) In what direction should it be advancing?

Casework is one of many ways of helping people with personal and social problems. These include psycho-analysis and other forms of psycho-therapy and group therapy, as well as counselling and social

* A revised version of 'What is Advanced Casework?' Published in New Barnett Papers No. I, *The Family in Modern Society*, Department of Social and Administrative Studies, Oxford University.

[1] A. Hunt, Paper in *Ventures in Professional Co-operation*, Association of Psychiatric Social Workers, London, 1960.

[2] M. A. G. Brown, 'A Review of Casework Methods,' Published as a supplement to *Case Conference*, February 1964, and in the present volume, pp. 11-37.

group work. Certain things are common to all these activities. They all involve a professional relationship, an interaction between one or more professional people with one or more people seeking help; and the quality of this interaction is generally believed to be of crucial importance to the helping process. They all involve insight on the part of the worker into personality, motivation and interaction, including their less rational and less conscious aspects; this insight includes awareness of one's own motivation and responses as well as those of the client. The practitioners of personal help have a number of techniques available: advice, reassurance, encouragement, explanation, questions, hints, practical help of various kinds, reminders of legal responsibility or other aspects of reality, sympathy, interpretation. I have deliberately left to the last the technique of interpretation, which is relatively new as a self-conscious device, but whose uses have been studied by analysts more intensively than those of the more traditional ways of helping have been studied by anyone, so that interpretation now tends to emerge as the figure against a ground of 'simple supportive and directive work'. I am also leaving aside the fascinating subjects of what I might call the 'near-interpretations' often used by caseworkers: the interpretive question, the interpretive comment, the interpretive reassurance. I will just give one instance of the interpretive comment. Sweet Polly Oliver in the ballad misses her soldier true-love so much that she disguises herself as a man and joins the Army in the hope of reunion. The sergeant appeals for a volunteer soldier nurse to attend to the sick Captain—who is none other than the missing true-love. In the face of the doctor's despair, Polly nurses her lover back to life— still incognito. Finally the doctor salutes her triumph with the remark: 'You have tended him as if you were his wife.' This unintentional interpretation is highly potent, for 'sweet Polly Oliver bursts into tears and told the good doctor her hope and her fears'. This enables him to do some effective marriage guidance.

To return to the variety of helping methods: I think it is true to say that the psycho-analysts, and some but not all psycho-therapists, try to keep the interaction component as muted and as standardized as possible, and to restrict it to the verbal level, and to the particular type of verbal response known as interpretation. The caseworker, on the other hand, has many more responses at her disposal, a collection of ingredients which she makes up into individual prescriptions as an adaptation to the needs of each client as she perceives them. We can see this as a continuum, a whole scale of responses, ranging from the interpretation (transference or extra-transference) which we have been learning from the analysts, to the largely non-verbal interaction in terms of practical help, gifts, loans, accompaniment to the doctor, the court or the delousing station which is appropriate to the 'problem family'. If we look at it this way, we by-pass all these meaningless discussions about whether casework can be combined with the exercise of authority or the giving of practical aid. Casework becomes a total interaction within which action is seen to have an aspect of non-verbal communication, and words to be one of the many forms of helpful activity. There should thus be no great difficulty in combining verbal and non-verbal aid, providing both these forms of communication are saying the same thing.

The Advanced Casework Course at the Tavistock Clinic, London, with which I am associated, was established at a time when Noel Hunnybun and her colleagues were much concerned with advancing in a certain direction; the understanding of the phenomena identified by Freud as transference and counter-transference as they occur within the setting of a casework relationship, and the use, within limits which were also subject to exploration, of techniques of transference interpretation. I believe that real and important advances were made. It was a difficult but worthwhile task to determine the level at which the un-analysed social worker could be trained to understand these phenomena, and the kind of interpretive comment which such workers could usefully make. I believe that *The Caseworker's Use of Relationship*,[1] by Hunnybun and Ferard, gives evidence of considerable progress in this direction. The question of the varying needs of different *clients* for more or less interpretive help, still requires a good deal of further exploration.

Although I believe the theory and practice of social work have been greatly enriched by this effort, I consider it unfortunate that advanced casework has come to be identified with this approach, since in view of the variety of personality and culture among clients and of their manifold needs, casework should be advancing on a much broader front than this. In fact, it undoubtedly is doing so, and the kind of work described by Betty Lloyd Davies[2] and Clare Winnicott[3] represents at least as great an advance in other directions, which should clearly be

[1] M. Ferard and N. Hunnybun, *The Caseworker's Use of Relationships*, Tavistock Publications, London, 1961.
[2] B. Lloyd Davies, 'Psychotherapy and Social Casework,' *In the Boundaries of Casework*, Association of Psychiatric Social Workers, London, 1957. Reprinted in *Relationship in Casework*, Association of Psychiatric Social Workers, London, 1964.
[3] C. Winnicott, 'Face to Face with Children,' in *New Thinking for Changing Needs*, Association of Social Workers, London, 1964, and in *Child Care and Social Work*, Codicote Press, Welwyn, 1964.

included in any account of advanced casework. The most advanced casework is that which best fits the need of the client in question, and we must not allow the labelling of courses to obscure this fact.

I believe in particular that the use of transference interpretation in casework is best adapted to the needs of neurotic clients, and that although psycho-analytic theory is equally illuminating in regard to psychotics and to all the varieties of character disorder (as well as to the emotional tangles of normal people) very different techniques are required in helping these kinds of person. In this context I would like to quote D. W. Winnicott:

'I think of each social worker as a therapist, but not as the kind of therapist who makes the correct and well-timed interpretation that elucidates the transference neurosis. Do this if you like, but your more important function is therapy of the kind that is always being carried on by parents in correction of relative failures in environmental provision. What do such parents do? They exaggerate some parental function and keep it up for a length of time, in fact until the child has used it up and is ready to be released from special care.'[1]

Here the emphasis is on the experiential or interactional aspect of the helping process rather than on the element of communication and insight. My own thinking began to move in this direction in 1956, when I published a paper called 'Transference and Reality in the Casework Relationship'.[2] Here I was beginning to formulate an account of casework process in terms of an experience in interaction, and I pointed out that stable parents provide a model which is more useful in many casework situations than that provided by psycho-analysis. I think we have made some progress in understanding our work in these terms and adapting techniques more deliberately to the needs of the individual client. I would like to quote from *The Essentials of Social Casework*.[3]

'The casework relationship is not the same for every client, but should, as far as possible, be adjusted to meet the varying need of different clients. One important function of the casework relationship is to

[1] D. W. Winnicott, 'The Mentally Ill in your Caseload,' in *New Thinking for Changing Needs*, Association of Social Workers, London, 1964.
[2] E. E. Irvine, 'Transference and Reality in the Casework Relationship,' *British Journal of Psychiatric Social Work*, Vol. III, No. 4, 1956. Reprinted in *Relationship in Casework*, Association of Psychiatric Social Workers, London, 1964, pp. 53-66; and in the present volume, pp. 108-123.
[3] *The Essentials of Social Casework*, Association of Psychiatric Social Workers, London, 1963, p. 2.

supply in some measure those experiences necessary for satisfactory emotional development, which have been lacking in the life of the individual client. Thus an inhibited and submissive client may need to be encouraged to speak his mind to the worker, and to express his feelings of criticism and dissatisfaction as a prelude to developing the ability to stand up for himself in other situations. On the other hand, a client whose pattern of behaviour is to control and exploit people until they eventually throw him over, may need to have a relationship with someone who resists all attempts to manipulate him, while remaining friendly and sympathetic. Thus the balance between firmness and permissiveness has to be finely adjusted to the needs of the client, and should not be influenced by the worker's own need, for example, to control situations himself, or to keep on the right side of everybody.'

There is no question of such work being easier or less 'advanced', and it often requires just as much dynamic insight into personality and motivation.

In 'Transference and Reality'[1] I confined my attention to the emotional interaction underlying various forms of verbal interchange. This I think we now understand more clearly, but there is still a need to apply the same kind of systematic analysis on the practical level. We need to look at the whole question of gifts and loans, not only as responses to material need, but to psychological need as well. Mrs Dockar-Drysdale, working in a boarding school for maladjusted children, and Dr J. Lomax-Simpson, a psychiatrist working with children in care, have both evolved interesting applications of D. W. Winnicott's concepts of maternal adaptation and transitional objects. Mrs Dockar-Drysdale writes of what she calls 'a localized adaptation' used in work with very disturbed children in a residential setting. Certain children are felt to need something which will give them a taste of the feelings of being understood and secure, which a mother's near-perfect adaptation to her tiny baby, gives him. Obviously a professional worker with responsibilities to other children cannot allow any one child to be dependent in just the same way as a baby, but some little ritual can be evolved which symbolises so much more—in one case it was the provision of a sweet of a certain special colour every day at the same time.[2] This sounds like a gimmick, but the choice of gift or service must arise directly out of a deep communion of child and adult,

[1] ibid.
[2] B. E. Dockar-Drysdale, 'The Provision of Primary Experience in a Therapeutic School.' Unpublished paper, 1964.

the symbol must be something they find together, or it will not symbolize anything, it will be just a feeble fobbing off of a hungry child. In this case his demands will not be abated, whereas if the symbol is rightly chosen, the child can bear to share his loved person with others for the rest of the day.

Dr Lomax-Simpson[1] has worked out something similar which helps her to provide through her relationship with children and adolescents a sense of deep security, even where contact is intermittent and not very frequent. With a girl who was leaving care she provided an artificial pearl necklace rather like one of her own, with a promise that she would always have it re-threaded. Thus at the same time she gave something of hers and a built-in device for renewing contact when necessary. With another child it might be something quite different, whose significance derives from some allusion to a meaningful shared experience—something like always remembering to provide strawberry jam when they have tea together. Some adult clients need birthday and Christmas cards in this way, or postcards during holidays. To quote my own work with a feeble-minded woman (mother of several disturbed children), I think the only really meaningful things which have happened between us have been on the plane of action. I went with her to visit her dying husband in hospital, and to his funeral. On many visits both before and after his death, I could do nothing but listen helplessly to the continuous quarrelling in the family. I gave presents of food at Christmas, redecorated the house a bit, took her shopping once on a Saturday morning, sorted out some muddles with the National Assistance Board and the Ministry of Pensions. After some years of this she presented me with four pillow-cases; soon afterwards, I lent her money to buy furniture, trusting her to pay it off by instalments; she managed to do so, and even offered on one occasion, when she was short at the time of my visit, to send it on by post; to my surprise and joy she actually did so.

Another client was angry and despairing, and never managed to make any real use of her weekly hour, beyond letting off a blast of impotent fury. I adapted to her need, as I perceived it, by giving her, without being asked, a second consecutive hour each week. This had several advantages on different levels. On the one hand, the longer period enabled her to relax after venting her more violent feelings, so that we could then have a calmer and more constructive discussion, in which some insight was developed. But just as important as anything

[1] J. N. Lomax-Simpson, 'Needs of the Child in Care,' *Case Conference*, Vol. X, No. 7, January 1964.

I said was the fact that I had seen her need and responded to it *without being asked*, since one of her problems was that nothing was any good if she had to ask for it. It was only later, when I judged her ready to be weaned back to a single hour, that I realized how apt this symbolic cliché was; my client wondered why she was so hungry all the time! Later, she brought me some little gifts, mostly small plants she had grown. Once, presenting a little cactus, she said: 'This is one of my babies.'!

Occasionally with psychotic patients I have found it was tremendously helpful to disregard our usual practice and give a little bit of factual information about myself. I realize that this is a rediscovery of something that other workers have been doing intuitively for years; but I think it needs integrating into our theoretical framework, so that we can understand and teach more clearly when this is helpful and when it is not.

We are becoming more aware and planful about our non-verbal communication, as described, for instance, in *The Canford Families*.[1] But the important distinction is really not between verbal and non-verbal, it is something about the way and the purpose with which language is used. Interpretive language is used to convey to the client something about himself, perhaps to help him communicate better with lost parts of himself, to win recognition for them. The other use of language is to communicate something about the worker's attitude, his concern, his sympathy, his empathic understanding, his hope, his acceptance. Ultimately, the aim of this too is to help the client recognize and take responsibility for disowned aspects of himself, those parts which he cannot himself accept until he has felt them accepted by someone whom he respects. These things can be communicated by words (in the right tone of voice) but also by smiles, by gestures and by behaviour, by scrupulous keeping of promises, by taking trouble or extra trouble, even by accepting a cup of tea—as one client said: 'What, in this awful house?'[2]

This brings us back to the home visit and the interview with several family members. These again are nothing new, but have tended of recent years to be regarded as unavoidable necessities which make it difficult to do proper casework. However, various writers have made us take a new look at these situations and recognize them as representing both a challenge and an opportunity. Challenging they certainly are,

[1] *The Canford Families*, Sociological Review, Monograph No. 6, University of Keele, December 1962.
[2] B. Day, 'Supportive Casework in an Authoritative Setting,' *Case Conference*, Vol. XI, No. 9, March 1965.

and it is tempting to try to create an individual interview situation by withdrawing with the client into another room, or to try and exclude one or more members of the family—e.g. children. Failing success in these manoeuvres, one may be tempted to regard the situation as an individual interview in trying circumstances. We naturally fear to get 'out of our depth' if we venture to interact with all the people present in a way which encourages free communication instead of trying to keep the conversation innocuous and the party clean. But these problems have been courageously tackled in various ways by various people, some of whom have attempted to describe their techniques. One of the authors of *The Canford Families*[1] describes a visit to a family where the parents had that morning destroyed a pet belonging to one of their children, and how the worker tried 'to convey that their different feelings are all legitimate and accepted'. E. M. Goldberg describes a more ambitious technique: 'using for one's interpretations the abundant supply of material from the past as well as from the present. . . . One tries to catch as much as possible of what is thrown around, showing the family members . . . what they were doing and have done to each other, how they misunderstood, misinterpreted and so on.'[2] This sounds more difficult (and therefore 'advanced') but I am not sure whether the art of non-verbal communication is not even more so— 'The use of action, symbol and inference rather than direct verbal expression.'[3]

Whether or not we visit the home, whether we work with two or more members of the family or whether we find a different worker for each member, we have to take steps to improve our understanding of family functioning—of the family as a system of interacting individuals. The Family Discussion Bureau has blazed a well-documented trail[4, 5] through studies of the marital relationship in terms of conscious adaptation and maladaptation and unconscious collusion through mutual projections and identifications. We still have to extend this type of analysis to include children. This is something we are working on.

I will briefly mention some final points. There has been a tendency to regard long-term intensive casework as more 'advanced' than short-

[1] ibid., p. 187.
[2] E. M. Goldberg, 'Parents and Psychotic Sons,' *British Journal of Psychiatric Social Work*, London, Vol. V, No. 4, 1960.
[3] *The Canford Families*, ibid., p. 170.
[4] Family Discussion Bureau, *Social Casework in Marital Problems*, Tavistock Publications, London, 1955.
[5] Family Discussion Bureau, *Marriage: Studies in Emotional Conflict and Growth*, Methuen, London, 1960.

contact work, which is often regarded as superficial, a necessary but unsatisfactory concession to pressing demands or adverse circumstances. These assumptions I am sure we have to revise. Skilled use of short contacts, especially in crisis situations, can be extremely effective —but to be effective it must be at least as highly skilled as so-called intensive work. We have a lot to learn about short-term focused work, the skill of helping the client just enough to restore or achieve adequate functioning in respect of the problem presented without opening up his problems in general and becoming sunk for years in the effort to resolve them. This I would regard as very advanced indeed. In work with the mentally ill we have a lot to learn about how to select the best focus for treatment (Waldron, 1961)[1] and how to identify the family member with whom it would be most profitable to invest one's major effort. We also have to learn to maintain a balanced concern for all members of the family, especially in situations where there is no team to take responsibility for different members. There is a real danger of helping our client at the expense of some other member of his family, or at least of ignoring the fact that his illness is disturbing relatives or children who may not get the help they need unless we do something about it.

These are only some of the directions in which we need to advance. Perhaps I can sum up the situation by saying that we need to develop more appropriate and effective techniques for all types of clients in all kinds of agency—for the clients of the family service units, of the special problem family caseworkers in public health, of the various voluntary and religious organizations (including the protective agencies) as well as for those of the child care and probation services, local authority mental health services, the child guidance clinic and the Family Discussion Bureau.

---

[1] F. E. Waldron, 'The Choice of Goals in Casework Treatment,' *British Journal of Psychiatric Social Work*, Vol. VI, No. 2, 1961.

3

THE GENERIC AND SPECIFIC IN SOCIAL CASEWORK RE-EXAMINED*

FLORENCE HOLLIS

THE student who majors in casework is expected upon graduation from a school of social work to take responsibility for the care of people who are in serious—sometimes in desperate—trouble. Often these are people who are at a point of crisis in their lives where what the caseworker does or fails to do may be decisive as to whether a child is to be brought up in hostile, neglectful turmoil or in the relative security of a foster or adoptive home; whether a marriage is to continue or be broken; whether or not a family is to be adequately clothed, sheltered, and fed; whether a mentally sick person is to reach a hospital for care or end his life in suicide; whether a patient is to undergo an operation for cancer or run away in fear from medical advice. Obviously, the caseworker cannot make such decisions for others, but the way in which he relates to and talks with people day in and day out plays a major part in determining whether clients take action towards a better life or a worse. Basic skill in casework treatment the school graduate must have; otherwise we have failed in preparing him for the immediate job that will be entrusted to him by the community. It is our responsibility through professional and other national organizations to see that this objective of social work education is amply met.

In reality, all fields of social work are reaching for the same objective —to man our agencies with workers of the highest possible quality. We have for many years been in agreement that this requires at least two years of graduate training. We are all in agreement that it is impossible to teach the student in these two years all that is needed for competent practice in any setting, and that at least two years of sub-

* Published in *Social Casework*, Vol. XXXVII, No. 5, May 1956; also published in *Social Casework in the Fifties*, Family Service Association of America, New York, 1962.

sequent practice under good supervision are needed before the average worker reaches mature competence. Some fields speak of 'internships'; many agencies have some form of post-graduate in-service staff training. There is increasing interest in formalized third-year and doctoral training programmes. At the same time the healthy emphasis on training for social work rather than narrowly for casework, on broad professional education rather than narrow technical training, is increasing. Thus it is imperative that we make the most of each educational hour and that we weigh carefully what can best be given in the basic Master's programme, and what can most safely be delayed for the worker's later development.

There is also general agreement, I think, that casework includes both generic and specific content and that both are important. Just as there is no doubt that certain generic content is basic to practice in all agencies, so it is also agreed that some content is specific to practice in certain types of agencies and not in others, and even that some content is specific to one agency and not to others. This fact, however, does not answer for us the questions of how much of this specific material can be taught in the Master's programme, in what units it is to be organized, and what methods are administratively and educationally best for assuring its teaching.

Before discussing some of the basic issues involved I should like to outline, as a frame of reference, the content that I should like to see included in the education of all caseworkers.

It should be kept in mind that the emphasis of this paper is on the training of the *caseworker*. Therefore, in what follows I am not attempting to discuss these issues as they apply to group work or other types of social work. First of all, I believe that casework is a *basic major* or area of concentration within social work education. Casework itself can be considered a specialization but I prefer to use the term 'major' instead of 'specialization' because of the present use of the term 'specialization' to describe the various subdivisions by setting of the total field of casework. Group work is another such area of concentration. Whether community organization, administration, and research are also basic majors is debatable. They are certainly processes within the field of social work, but perhaps as majors they represent content to be studied at an advanced level after one of the basic methods has been mastered.

Every student preparing to practice in the casework field should master the broad social work curriculum as well as the content in his own major field. This broad social work curriculum should provide the student with knowledge of the field of social work as a whole, its historical development, and its current place and function in our culture. It should inform him about the present structure of social services, public and private. It should orient him to the philosophical premises upon which social work rests and to his role as a practitioner who carries responsibility for the welfare of other human beings. It should give him knowledge of the social, physical, and psychological factors in the development and adjustment of the individual. It should equip him with beginning skills in research. In addition to undertaking this broad social work curriculum, the student majoring in casework should study intensively the process of social casework itself; the group work student, the process of social group work; and so on.

It is not necessary in developing the subject of this paper to discuss in detail the actual structure of courses in which all this subject matter would be taught, but only to comment on areas that have been emphasized as requirements for specialization. I would suggest for all casework majors a one-semester course in medical problems and two-semester courses on aspects of the dynamics of behaviour with one or two more courses on this subject available as electives in the second year. In social casework itself I would suggest four semesters of basic casework courses with additional courses available as electives. I would prefer to see casework major students spend three days a week in field work —on the assumption that this would occupy half their actual study time—spending this in two agencies in successive years, preferably one in a primary social work setting and one in a secondary setting— an agency that has as its basic function somethng other than social work. In all field work I would like to see attention given not only to direct work with clients but also to aspects of practice which draw upon the subject matter of other than casework courses in the curriculum.

Where would specific content be placed in such a curriculum? A variety of patterns is possible. With proper planning most of the specific content can be incorporated into the basic courses. A good deal of it would be placed in the casework sequence and some in other areas of basic content—that is, community organization content in the community organization course, group work aspects in group work, administration in the administration course, and so on. Additional specific emphasis could be given in elective courses open to all casework students. These elective courses would, perhaps, resemble present settings courses, or on the other hand might take on a new pattern, drawing upon similar specific content found in different settings.

D

Let us look first at the so-called generic casework courses. We have learned that it is not only undesirable, but impossible, to teach generic content divorced from specific content. A properly constructed basic casework sequence draws its materials from all types of agency settings. Inevitably, cases reveal specific as well as generic factors. Take a child placement case. Before the decision to place the child is made and the specific foster home is decided upon, a social study has to be undertaken which differs very little from that made in a family agency dealing with parent-child adjustment, in a child guidance clinic, in a hospital offering service to a child with a long-standing illness affecting his family relationships, or in a school setting where intensive help is given to the child who is truanting. Indeed, perhaps some of the differences that do appear should not be there and would not be there had there been more cross-fertilization between casework settings.

But, you say, there are other special features about the application for placement of a child: the parent is in conflict about placement, guilty about it, protective, and reluctant to talk. Are not partially rejecting parents and parents unable to care adequately for their children almost always guilty and reluctant to face, or talk frankly about painful aspects of their lives, no matter to what type of agency they turn for help?

But, the argument continues, sometimes the parent does not even come voluntarily; he is referred because someone else thinks his child should be placed. Have you ever read about the involuntary nature of *medical* referrals? That it is often the doctor, not the patient, who requests the medical social worker? In *psychiatric* social work, what of the relative of the patient? What about 'aggressive' work in the *family* field? 'Intrusive'[1] casework in the psychiatric field?

The advocate of specialities contends that one must understand the child's feeling about *separation*. Indeed, it is important to understand that, and a child's placement record is a very good resource in teaching about it, because child welfare has developed good content around that problem which the rest of us very much need to know. Several writers in the medical field have attested to the contribution of child welfare to their understanding of the reaction of the child to hospital and convalescent care. What about the separation factor in the school phobia? In prolonged parental illness? In desertion by a parent? In divorce? In death?

---

[1] Rudolf F. Boquet, 'The Use of an "Intrusive" Technique in Casework with Chronic Mentally Ill Patients,' *Journal of Psychiatric Social Work*, Vol. XXIV, No. 1 (1954), pp. 31-5.

If you read the articles describing the content specific to each of the major fields, the thought constantly occurs—'But this happens in other fields, too.' One article states that the medical social worker has to learn to work with patients from the upper income brackets. What about child welfare work with adoptive and foster parents? What about the fee-paying cases in family agencies? Another writer states that the medical social worker has great opportunity to work with incipient problems. What about the public welfare worker or the school social worker?

It is true that certain agencies deal repetitively with certain types of problems and therefore accumulate detailed knowledge about these problems and facility in dealing with them. This is true, for instance, of the child placement agency in respect to problems of placement, the selection of foster homes, work with foster parents; of the state hospital and sometimes of the out-patient psychiatric clinic in their work with psychotics. It is true for the child guidance clinic in its work with certain types of disturbed children; for the hospital in relation to physical illness; for the private family agency in treatment of marital problems and problems of parent-child adjustment; for the public assistance agency in problems of self-support; and so on.

This greater skill is acquired by years of practice and should be fed back into the main stream of casework, since giving help with human problems is not confined to specific agency settings. Problems are multiple. The medical worker's problem may begin with a broken leg, but before the work is ended it may very well turn into a problem of school adjustment. Schizophrenia is appearing with increasing frequency among the clients of family agencies, partly because patients in partial remission are encouraged by hospitals to return to the community, and partly because caseworkers are better able to recognize schizophrenia in its incipient and less severe forms. The client, to be sure, does not come for treatment of his schizophrenia. He may come because of an unsuccessful marriage, but knowledge of schizophrenia and of casework with this specific type of mental illness is essential to the proper handling of the client. The student who has studied a case of schizophrenia from the files of a psychiatric agency puts that knowledge to good use when he meets the same problem in a family, medical, or child welfare setting. The graduate employed in a veterans' psychiatric clinic may be greatly strengthened in playing his part on the clinical team if he has studied cases from a family agency which have revealed the degree of distortion sometimes present in descriptions given of each other by husband and wife in marital conflict situations.

The student years are pre-eminently the years for the student to learn from the special, the specific knowledge of a great *variety* of agencies. A number of workers never again will have this opportunity, since they will remain in one type of agency throughout their working lives, even though the majority of workers eventually practice in a variety of settings. Graduates will have plenty of time in which to build up skill in the specifics of their own setting, but this may be the only time that they will have a chance to study what caseworkers in other agency settings have discovered and developed. There are much greater advantages to be gained from exposing the student to the rich specifics of a variety of settings than from concentrating in the second year on the one setting in which he may spend the rest of his professional career.

The required basic casework sequence could well be supplemented by elective courses that will give the student a chance for concentration upon some aspect of casework in which he is particularly interested or which the faculty is particularly well equipped to teach. These courses might or might not fall strictly along field lines. There would be advantages in experimenting with different patterns. One of the advantages of our present settings courses is that they give the student a chance to study certain types of problems more repetitively than is possible in the basic courses which emphasize variety of problems rather than concentrated comparative study of cases having similar features. In our present family casework course, for instance, we have a number of marriage counselling cases. By seeing several different types of reactions to the same social adjustment problem, students deepen their understanding of marriage adjustment in a way that goes beyond what they can do in the basic course. A preferable alternative to building these elective courses around settings might be to build them around a series of cases having a common denominator either in the social problem or in clinical diagnosis.

Thus far I have neglected teamwork. Collaboration with other disciplines and the general problem of fitting into a secondary type of setting (to use the terminology of Helen Perlman[1]) are the most frequently cited hallmarks of 'specialization'. School social work, medical social work, psychiatric social work, and probation and parole all meet this problem in varying ways. Relationships between professions

[1] Helen Harris Perlman, 'Generic Aspects of Specific Casework Settings,' *Social Service Review*, Vol. XXIII, No. 3 (1949), p. 295.

are complicated and in a secondary setting they differ from those in a primary setting, but they do belong to the same genus if not the same species. Helen Perlman has already dealt with this problem very well in her article on the University of Chicago curriculum.[1] She points out that general principles are involved in such staff relationships, which take different forms in different types of agencies.

This is an area in which comparative study might be particularly fruitful. Administrative courses might well be enriched by the analysis of this and other types of administrative relationships in different agencies. Study of the psychiatric collaboration common in the family agency, for instance, might have much to offer to practice in secondary settings. Indeed, I know of one very good psychiatric hospital that now uses two kinds of psychiatric teamwork. The conventional type is used for work with the patient, but in addition to this a senior psychiatrist is made available to staff members of the social work department as a consultant on work with relatives. The team relationship here has many similarities to that ordinarily found in primary settings. Certain aspects of interdisciplinary collaboration of course inevitably appear also in the basic casework sequence, for they are a part of the specifics of many cases from all fields. This same principle of incorporation of pertinent material about settings could well be applied to other courses in the curriculum, particularly The Field of Social Work, Community Organization, and Public Welfare. These all deal in one way or another with resources in relation to need and with the structure of social work fields. Restudy of their content with this in mind might lead to a sequence comparable to the basic casework sequence and the human behaviour sequence.

It is obvious, of course, that it is in field work that the student learns most about the specific aspects of any particular setting. When a student spends three days a week for eight months in an agency, he is given substantial opportunity for drill in whatever is special to that agency and the field of which it is a part.

On close examination, the organization of teaching along field lines does not appear to have too much logic. There is just as much difference between the knowledge needed in different types of agencies in the same field as there is between agencies in different fields. Some child guidance clinics and mental hygiene agencies, for instance, are closer in both structure and type of problem dealt with to the family agency than to the state hospital. The out-patient psychiatric clinic is

[1] ibid., pp. 293-301.

closer to the out-patient medical clinic than to the child guidance agency. The work of the children's worker in an institution may be closer to that of the medical worker in a children's convalescent home or a psychiatric worker in a residential treatment centre than to that of a worker in a foster home agency. And certainly it is no longer true that one setting requires greater knowledge of the dynamics of human behaviour than another. In a workshop for psychiatric social workers and family and children's workers in New York in 1953, it was pointed out[1] that the family worker takes more responsibility for diagnosis than the average psychiatric social worker does. There are many psychiatric settings in which the caseworker is excluded from the use of treatment methods commonly required in many family agencies. I do not mean by this to imply that family casework requires more skill than psychiatric, but merely to call attention to the fact that, in reality, differences in specifics do not follow field lines alone.

I should like to turn now to consideration of some of the specific requirements that are at present in force in many schools of social work. For example, a frequent requirement is that the student's second-year placement be in his specialization. At first thought this seems reasonable enough, but it is based on the assumption that the student knows in what field he wants to specialize before he enters the school, so that the school can assign him to a different field for his first-year placement. Sometimes this plan can be followed, but often the student discovers his interest in a certain field only after he has had experience in it quite by chance in his first year. More and more we are learning that, although all fields prefer second-year students, they all are able to provide a substantial number of first-year placements. Beginning work and advanced work definitely do not follow field lines.

Many considerations other than choice of field enter into assignment of students to second-year placements. Quality of supervision is certainly one of these. It not infrequently happens that the best supervisor for a particular student is to be found in a field other than the one he thinks he wants to enter. Should he be advised to take a less suitable placement in order to meet specific field requirements even though that means that he will be less well prepared to practice in that field? If a superabundance of good placements existed in all fields, some of these specifications would be more practical than they actually are. I think we can assume that a student who knows what type of agency he wants to work in and who has not already had a first-year

---

[1] 'Current Trends in Psychiatric Settings and in Family and Children's Agencies,' *Journal of Psychiatric Social Work*, Vol. XXIV, No. 3 (1955), p. 163.

placement in it, will choose this kind of agency for his second year, other things being equal. We do not have to legislate this. If other things are not equal, they should be given consideration and the student, upon graduation, should not be handicapped in getting a job in the field of his choice because it seemed better from an educational viewpoint for him to receive his field training in another setting.

Similar considerations apply to the popular requirement that the student do his thesis in the field in which he proposes to work. By and large the student will choose such a subject but sometimes there are good reasons for his pursuing some other line of investigation. He may know of some particularly interesting group project in progress. He may have become especially interested in some problem encountered in his first year of study which he can profitably pursue further. Why should we legislate on a matter like this? Are there not enough rigidities in life without creating unnecessary ones?

Another proposed requirement is that the student take a settings course in the field in which he intends to work. Again it is true that, other things being equal, a student will elect courses according to his interests. He will not need to be coerced into doing so. If he does not choose a course related to his vocational plans it is probably because he believes the course is not as well taught or does not have as valuable content as others with which it is competing. Is it not better to know this situation exists so that it can be improved, rather than to obscure the matter by requiring the student to take such a course? Such a requirement also, of course, makes it extremely difficult to experiment with new curriculum patterns and creates vocational handicaps for the student graduating from a smaller school, which cannot offer a large number of special courses.

Most shortsighted of all is the policy of making faculty appointments and faculty assignments primarily along settings lines. This policy is based on the theory that, to train students who are to enter a particular field, a school must have a faculty member who is qualified for membership in the professional organization in that field (or, to bring us up to date, for membership in that section of NASW). Since, thus far, only three professional groups have pressed for this policy, some of the larger schools could comply. But if this idea is pushed, why will not other fields ask for the same recognition? Ultimately, then, each school would need also a family caseworker, a child welfare worker, a delinquency worker. And then, why not a rehabilitation instructor, perhaps one in geriatrics, and in whatever new fields emerge in the rest of the century? It would be a practical impossibility for all but the largest schools to meet all the claims for special treatment which could, with equal validity, be made. Already smaller schools, instead of being able to choose faculty on the basis of scholarship, competence in practice, and teaching skill, are having to give preference to candidates who have technical specializations in the three fields represented by membership organizations. This is wrong, very wrong, and inevitably it will lead to less well prepared graduates for *all* settings.

Once on a faculty, such a specialized instructor is expected to carry as his assignment all field work placements within his type of setting. This seems logical only because we have all been brought up with stereotypes about field lines and we are caught in the mesh of our own errors. At the New York School of Social Work we have now had three years of experimentation in assigning faculty members to field placements in agency settings in which they have never practiced. Inevitably this plan called for an initial learning period for the adviser before all the nuances of the new type of agency could be understood. But did we have complaints from agencies on this ground? On the contrary, agencies have been enriched and faculty members have been greatly broadened in their knowledge and perspective by this cross-fertilization. In fact, this is one of the best ways of improving the basic casework courses.

If we insist on keeping ourselves in iron-clad isolated compartments, of course we shall continue to be ignorant both of the extent to which we are now similar and of whatever content is specific in any field other than our own. But why should we allow ourselves to be caught in this growth-restricting, isolationist trap? We need to combine our strength in order to bring all caseworkers to a higher level of competence so that clients and patients will be met with thorough psychosocial understanding and adequate treatment skills, whatever the agency their self-recognized problems initially lead them to.

Why is this objective more likely to be met by emphasizing basic training than training for special settings? Because there is now more than enough basic social work and basic casework content to fill the two years of training for the Master's degree. Because the student is best prepared for actual practice when he knows something of the specifics of several settings rather than concentrating on one. Because it is better to avoid unnecessary rigidities in training. Because schools of social work can offer better professional education when they are not fettered in choice of teaching personnel and in the assignment of faculty responsibilities by settings requirements.

For all these reasons, I believe that we must continue along the path we have so recently chosen of subordinating our old separatist loyalties to the task of building a profession fit to serve the hurt and the troubled wherever they are to be found.

4

THE ROLE CONCEPT AND SOCIAL CASEWORK: SOME EXPLORATIONS

THE 'SOCIAL' IN SOCIAL CASEWORK*

HELEN HARRIS PERLMAN

I FIRST became interested in role about fifteen years ago, at a party. It was a square-dancing party, large enough so that many of us were strangers to one another. Within one square was a man who was the despair of us all. When the caller cried 'right', this man went left; when we were to stop, he skipped; 'skip' and he stopped; when it was 'swing your partner', he stood stock-still; he fumbled, stumbled, collided—by the end of the round he was miserable, and so were the rest of us. One of us went to our host to ask who this poor misfit was. 'Oh, that one,' he said, 'he's Mr X—the famous physicist.'

You know what happened. Our perceptions did a somersault. We had seen Mr X in his role as a dancing partner—he was inept, apologetic, bumbling to the point of stupidity. In his role as physicist, internationally recognized, he was keen, serenely confident, respected, and related to by others as a genius. And upon the somersault of our perceptions came the adaptation of our attitudes and behaviour toward Mr X. Warm indulgence took the place of mild annoyance; eager helpfulness replaced bland acceptance.

This, and less dramatic instances like it, set me to wondering. Which, I asked myself, is the real Mr X? Which is the real me—or you? How much effect does a particular role we carry have upon the manifestations of our personalities? One role calls certain behaviour and personality attributes to the fore and subordinates others; another role, undertaken in another hour, may make those subordinated behaviours dominant. How many of us, I wondered, know ourselves or can describe ourselves as persons without reference to our roles? And when in one's role as

* Published in Social The Service Review, Vol. XXXV, No. 4, December 1961.

caseworker, I thought, one sees an applicant or client, does one see him as a total personality? Is it possible that the role of applicant and, later, of client brings particular kinds of behaviour to the fore? Then a number of problems and recurrent questions in casework practice began to cast themselves into role questions. In our work with families, when we have a primary client, such as a hospitalized patient or an institutionalized child, how do we deal with family members? In what role do we cast them? Are they co-treaters? secondary clients? informants on call? And in what role versus caseworker, versus primary client, do they perceive themselves? And what do these perceptions have to do with how they act and what they expect of themselves and of the caseworkers? Or in work with foster parents: would it be useful to define for ourselves and for them and thus for the child in placement what the role of foster parent requires and demarcates? Is the foster parent, to the caseworker, a colleague? to the child, 'a new mommy' or some lesser kin, or—? Is he supposed—since every role contains expectation—to love freely, but not too much? to want the child feelingly, but only until the agency rings the bell for ending? to be parent—yet not quite? 'treater'—yet not exactly? Might some of these placement problems yield to solution if they were examined as role problems?

The caseworker himself has many problems to solve in regard to his identity. In a secondary setting, who and what is he? What is his difference from and likeness to the other professional helpers with whom he works? In any setting, every caseworker knows the conflicts inherent in his being charged with professional responsibility and held to employee accountability. Would analysis of collaborative relationship problems and supervisor-worker relationships be facilitated if they were examined within the framework of role?[1]

These—and a host of like questions—led me to more intensive exploration of role ideas and their possible usefulness in casework. I have allowed myself this personalized and informal introduction simply to indicate that what I am about to set down began and evolved in everyday personal and professional experience. Certain perspectives and problems pushed for greater clarity, the concept of role offered a framework within which to think, and thus I began to examine the ideas inherent in that concept. Without that professional motivation and discontent and without a matrix of reflected-upon experience, it

---

[1] On the subject of social casework role as perceived by the applicant to a social agency, see Helen Harris Perlman, 'Intake and Some Role Considerations,' *Social Casework*, Vol. XLI, No. 4 (April 1960), 171-7.

might have been a sterile and rugged pursuit to study the abstract and sometimes abstruse social science literature on role theory. Moreover, an exploration into new ideas is actually a personal experience. One comes out of such a pursuit not as out of a laboratory where tests have been applied and one may say, 'It is a fact that . . .' Coming out of an exploration of ideas, one can only say, 'It seems to me . . .' or 'This is how it looks from my particular perspective . . .' or 'This is how I came to believe, though I do not yet know . . .'

The insistent question that I tried to hold before me as I read and thought about 'role' was this: What value does role hold in general for casework theory and, specifically, for actual casework practice?

Among some of the basic questions in social casework are two that have long concerned us all. One is, What is 'social' about social casework? The other stems from this: What is 'social diagnosis'?

In 1952, in an informal talk to a small group, I suggested that we 'put the social back in social casework'.[1] Had I been pressed at the time to say how to do this, I would have had to confess that I had very little idea. All I knew was that I was struggling in an inchoate way to find our special identity as social caseworkers. It was a struggle made all the more acute by a growing recognition that much of what I understood about people and their psychodynamics was understood by several other helping professions; that much of what I knew how to do to influence people's attitudes and behaviours was known and being done by other helping professions; that counsellors on all sorts of problems were becoming so numerous that half the population, it seemed, was counselling the other half—and that whether you were a 'caseworker', a 'counsellor', or a 'psychotherapist' depended more on your fashion sense than on your sense of special role. Yet, if one called one's self a 'social caseworker', it was imperative to be able to say what one's particular professional focus or competence area was, and why this was subsumed and supported under 'social work'. I became aware that many other social caseworkers were likewise concerned with this problem because the phrase 'putting the social back in social work' became all but a professional shibboleth.

My 'quest for identity' and for the place of 'social' pushed me to set forth several propositions. Because I cannot yet state them better than I did then, I quote from a paper I presented in 1952:

'The problem which a client brings to a social agency is perceived by

[1] ' "Free Association on Problems of Child Welfare": Putting the Social Back in Social Casework,' *Child Welfare*, XXXI (July 1952), pp. 8-9, 14.

him to be a problem in his social adjustment. It may be caused by a breakdown of normal sources of social sustenance, or it may be caused by the malfunctioning of the person himself; but in either case *the client sees and feels his problem in terms of social maladjustment* because it makes itself known to him as he *plays out his social roles* and engages in his social tasks. Even when, as a disturbed personality, he is at the very heart of his problem, he rarely comes to the social agency saying, "I myself, need help." He says, rather, "I need help in *relation to* my unhappy marriage, my bad child, my mother's interferences, my school work." He seeks a social agency because he assumes that it will relate to his social difficulty, to remove it or provide him with some way of coping with it. When other persons—laymen, teachers, doctors, psychiatrists—refer clients to social agencies, they think of this source of help, not because they perceive that the person is "sick" or "desperate" or "bad", but because they perceive him in a social situation to which those feelings and actions are related. And in the final appraisal as to whether or not the client has been helped, neither the client nor the worker nor the referral source ask whether all hazards to adjustment have been removed, or whether all emotional conflicts have been ironed out. The appraisal is rather in terms of whether the *client's ability to carry his social roles and his normal life-functions* has been reasonably restored or bettered. This says, then, that as the client and the community view it, *the person in interaction with some problematic aspect of his social reality is the focus of the social caseworker's concerns.*[1]

If this proposal has validity—that the expectation from client and community is that the social caseworker's particular job is to help people who are experiencing maladjustments in their social functioning, which is to say in their person-to-person, person-to-group, person-to-situation transactions—then it suggests some rough boundary lines for social casework's special knowledge and functions. These boundaries, while they do not offer exclusivity to social casework, do demarcate where its particular competence and responsibility lie. They demarcate a focus upon the human being in his current problematic functioning, in his troubled interaction between himself and at least one other person, and/or between himself and the environmental forces and instruments created or controlled by other people. This 'field' of interaction is, by definition, 'social'.

Included in this proposal also was the idea of social role. I had equated it with social functioning, and, while I had some uneasy question

[1] 'Social Components of Casework Practice,' in *Social Welfare Forum, 1953*, pp. 130-1. (Italics added.) Later, in 'Psychotherapy and Counseling: Some Distinctions in Social Casework,' *Annals of the New York Academy of Sciences*, Vol. LXIII (November 7 1955), pp. 386-95, these ideas were given some further development.

about whether they were fully synonymous, I did not pursue this but turned instead to work at what seemed to be a more perplexing problem: Was *all* of a client's social functioning to be considered within the caseworker's purview? If a client functioned as a father, a husband, a factory worker, a union steward, a son-in-law, did all these areas of social interaction call for appraisal? Obviously the caseworker's focus would be upon the ones in which problems were being encountered. But suppose problems permeated the person's functioning?

For some time I did not see the connection between role and partialization of the client's and caseworker's task. I worked, rather, on the problem of how to find diagnostic and treatment focus when, as the caseworker grows more knowledgeable, he sees so much more complexity in his cases. I came to the idea of the 'problem-to-be-worked',[1] which is simply a proposal that at any given time in a case some particular problem (or problem cluster) must be in the centre of the caseworker-client attention. During that hour or phase of treatment, other problems may have to be given side-line attention or held in abeyance.

The problem-to-be-worked in any given case at any given time may be so self-evident, so spontaneously agreed upon between client and caseworker, that it needs no finding. It is there, central and pressing. But there are many situations in which a complex network of problems confuses both caseworker and client. Where to begin? Where to focus? Among all the problems here—Jeanie's health, Jackie's truancy, Mr James's alcoholism, Mrs James's distracted housekeeping, the inadequate income and worse-than-inadequate management—which? Elsewhere I have suggested several criteria for priorities.[2] The most telling of them is the criterion of the client's own idea of what, at the moment, hurts him most, what he sees as his uppermost problem ('uppermost', not 'basic'), what he feels and thinks he wants help with. Almost always in the social agency this will take the form of some impaired and frustrating interaction between himself and another person or persons, or between himself and some events or conditions.

---

[1] I owe the useful phrase, 'problem-to-be-worked' (at any given time), to Mary Burns, professor of casework at the University of Michigan, who coined it when, in a doctoral seminar, we were struggling to define the difference between what a caseworker may see and understand and what he does. Earlier I had called this partialized problem the 'unit for work' (*Social Casework: A Problem-solving Process* (Chicago: University of Chicago Press, 1957), p. 29). Later, I used this idea of problem-to-be-worked as a way of delimiting family diagnosis ('Family Diagnosis: Some Problems,' in *Casework Papers, 1958* (New York: Family Service Association of America, 1958), pp. 5-17, and in *Social Welfare Forum, 1958*, pp. 122-34).
[2] See *Social Casework: A Problem-solving Process*, pp. 29-33.

The problem may, indeed usually will, have many facets. But it is most likely to be felt and expressed as a problem in one major aspect of his social interaction. In this aspect he is unable to be or to do what is expected or required of him (by others) or what he desires for himself (and others). He is, in short, unable to carry some vital social role.

What this suggests, then, is that the problem-to-be-worked between a social caseworker and his client, different as it will be for every case, will be a problem of undertaking, carrying, or gaining gratification in some necessary social role. As I recognized this, it became clear to me that 'social functioning' is an omnibus term covering the totality of roles any person carries at one time in his life, and that the caseworker's concentrated efforts, both diagnostic and treatment, at any given time must be upon the role in which difficulty is felt and manifest.[1]

How is 'the role in which difficulty is felt and manifest' different from, say, the problem that the client is having and feeling? Now it becomes necessary to examine the concept of role for its content.

Apparently social scientists have arrived at no definition of role that suits all tastes and contingencies.[2] So perhaps a caseworker may dare his own definitions, related to social casework's purposes and developed out of casework observation and experience with large numbers of people in troubled social relationships.

We are accustomed, in social casework, to thinking that the ways in which each of us relates to another or to a group of others is the expression of our own personality. This is demonstrably so. Yet our self-expressions in relation to others do not occur in hit-or-miss,

[1] I am indebted to two social work writers for their signal contributions in casting social casework thinking into a framework of role concepts—Henry Maas and Werner Boehm. The latter, in Vol. X of the 'Social Work Curriculum Study,' *The Social Casework Method in Social Work Education* (New York: Council on Social Work Education, 1959), suddenly identified for me the fact that 'role' and 'social functioning' are not synonymous, when he wrote, 'Social functioning, then, is the sum of the roles performed by a person,' and when he went on to say that one value in the role concept is that it 'permits identification of affected areas of social functioning'—that is to say, it enables the caseworker to differentiate between those areas of social functioning that are impaired and those in which reasonable balance is being maintained. See especially pp. 95-103.
Boehm's formulations, further developed, seem to derive from those of Maas, which were published earlier, but which I came on later. See 'Social Casework,' in *Concepts and Methods of Social Work*, ed. Walter Friedlander (New York: Prentice-Hall, 1958), chap. ii.
Perhaps this is the place to suggest that these two reading references offer the most ready and compact formulations of the possible relationships between role concepts and casework.
[2] For an account of a survey of the literature with reference to the role concept see Lionel J. Neiman and James W. Hughes, 'The Problem of the Concept of Role: A Re-Survey of the Literature,' in *Social Perspectives on Behaviour*, ed. Herman D. Stein and Richard A. Cloward (Glencoe, Ill.: Free Press, 1958).
The reader who wishes to study the role concept—a real prerequisite, I believe, to its incorporation into casework—will find selected references at the end of this article.

impulsive ways (except for the emotionally blind), nor do they occur in complete spontaneity. Our relationships with other people and to social circumstances occur in certain patterned ways. That is, our individual, personal ways of communicating are for the most part contained within, coloured by, and fashioned by certain over-all, socially determined, and organized patterns of expected behaviour. These patterns of expected behaviour—and by 'behaviour' we mean not only what is done but also the accompanying affects—are called 'roles'. Social roles mark out what a person in a given social position and situation is expected to be, to act like, and to feel like and what the other(s) in relation to him are expected to be, to act like, and to feel like. Such prescriptions are very general, to be sure, and, as Jessie Bernard has aptly put it, they usually allow for a good deal of 'ad libbing' within the script. But any observer of human behaviour knows that the ways in which we function in our love and friendship lives and in our work lives, our relationships with students, colleagues, celebrities, bus drivers, family members, doctors, are all determined not only by our personalities, but also by our notion of what we and they are supposed to be and do in relation to one another. Our actions are heavily determined by our ideas of role requirements or expectations.

Our behaviour in every social situation may be said to be selected and shaped by three dynamic factors:

1. Our needs and drives—what we want, consciously or unconsciously.

2. Our notions and feelings about the mutual obligations and expectations that have been invested (by custom, precept, and so on) in the particular status and functions we carry.

3. The compatability or conflict between our conceptions of reciprocal obligations and expectations and the conceptions of the other person(s) with whom we are in interaction.

The reader will be aware that our casework analyses of clients' behaviour have tended to be more focused upon (1) than upon (2) or (3). Items (2) and (3) express the effect of role on behaviour, and it is these ideas, I submit, that need our present careful consideration. For we know it to be true of ourselves that, when we find ourselves in a social situation in which behavioural expectations (role) are not clear, we fumble in trial-and-error adaptation. When we are clear what requirements are, but find that they run counter to our drives and needs, we feel conflicted. When our interpretation of requirements is different from the interpretation made by the person with whom we interact, both conflict and confusion may result. When requirements themselves are ill-defined or inadequately defined, we may feel and act in diffuse and inept ways.

When, on the other hand, we have the knowledge, the capacity, and the motivation to carry the requirements inherent in a role we have undertaken, we are said to be, and we actually feel, 'well-balanced'; we are 'effective' in our social functioning. Freud, you remember, when asked what marked the mature man, said he must be able to love and to work. In working we carry our task-centred roles. In loving we carry our relationship-centred roles. In the combination of both are to be found all the facets of man's social functioning.

I said before that 'social functioning' is an omnibus term. It expresses an idea of role clusters because in the course of any day's social functioning each of us carries a number of roles. Some roles are in the ascendancy at a given time, and others are subordinate. Their positions may be reversed, depending on time, place and circumstance. Some of these daily roles are fairly mechanical, 'outer-layer' operations, easily put on and taken off. But other roles we perform are deeply invested with feeling and are embraced by the personality because they meet or are expected to meet essential personal needs, because they provide or promise gratifications, because they embody emotionally and socially valued positions. It is when one of these latter roles is threatened or undermined that casework help is sought; it is with these that the caseworker is concerned. Other roles or aspects of the client's social functioning may remain relatively intact, although psychological energies and manoeuvring will be involved in their management. The caseworker's diagnostic eye will sweep across and take account of those aspects of social functioning in which the person retains relative mastery. But his diagnostic concentration will be upon the particular role(s), within total social functioning, in which the person is having trouble. This will give boundary, focus, and direction to the caseworker's activity.

But back to the question: What does this idea of role hold that the idea of some uppermost problem does not provide? Although the concept of role has been defined in tens upon tens of ways, the social scientists who have developed and used the concept seem to be agreed that 'social role' always implies at least four 'constant elements'. These are the constant elements, the regularities of content that make it possible for us to view a person's role performance in an organized, regularized way. Just as the triad concept of id-ego-superego offers us a famework within which to view many variations of personality structure and functioning, so that role concept offers—or promises—a framework within which to view and examine the many variations of social functioning.

When role is understood it regularly forces our attention upon these aspects of social behaviour that are of primary import to a caseworker:

1. *Role implies that certain activities and behaviours are requisite to any given status.* They may be required by common agreements in a given culture or within given social units (community or family unit) or they may be attributed to the particular position by role participants. In any case, the fact for the caseworker regularly to ascertain in any analysis of a client's role problem is: depending on the role problem being examined, what and how does this person do, what activities does he carry out? (in his operations as a father? a husband? an employee?)

2. *Role implies interaction.* No role can be carried alone. (Even a hermit's mental world is probably peopled; at least, it is *from* others that he separates himself.) Every role involves one or more *others.* For the caseworker, this means that any problem identified as a role problem must be viewed as an interaction situation. The role of mother includes the reciprocal one of child; husband, of wife; student, of teacher; wage-earner, of employer or boss or 'company'; and so on. It signals to us awareness that others than the individual client who presents himself will be involved in causing or affecting his problem, involved in its solution or outcome, involved in its consequences. Therefore it alerts us to the necessity to consider those others, to consider those others not only in our diagnosis but in treatment. It forces us to view the person not as an entity alone but always as involved in an inter-action process, and thus to consider whether and how to deal with the other(s) involved.

Family diagnosis with which casework practitioners today are widely concerned is probably not possible except by use of role ideas. Yester-day's effort at family diagnosis was an addition of appraisals of individual personalities which had an annoying way of refusing to result in a sum or conclusion. Today's family diagnosis is an effort— not yet achieved for the most part—to assess a configuration of forces, patterned not simply by the personalities involved but also by the roles in relation to one another. One of the major differences between yesterday's and today's family treatment is that we are now reaching out to deal not with all family members but with those whose roles seem vital to the problem-to-be-worked.[1]

[1] For an elaboration of this point, see Perlman, 'Family Diagnosis: Some Problems,' op. cit., and 'Family Diagnosis in Cases of Illness and Disability,' in *Family Centred Social Work in Illness and Disability* (Monograph IV (New York: National Association of Social Workers, 1961)).

3. *Role implies that there are certain 'social expectations' and social norms* for these activities and interactions between and among human beings. As soon as this is said, we face the persistent and valid arguments that for some social behaviours there are no norms, that in a rapidly changing society norms are in flux, that class and culture subgroups in a society have differing norms, and so forth. These arguments are all true, and all important to take into account. Yet if the caseworker is to avoid paralysis and not himself become a victim of normlessness, he must take measure of those norms and standards that are considered acceptable and desirable by the community which his agency, and therefore he, represents. To do this is not as stultifying or as regimenting as we sometimes pretend it is. First of all, a norm or standard of human behaviour is not a sharply defined point. It represents, rather, a range of 'usualness', a sketched model. Within such a range or model many variations and interpretations of behaviour are socially acceptable. 'Good social functioning' and 'good role performance' can be assessed only on a continuum from what seems socially constructive to what seems socially acceptable to what seems or is unacceptable; from what seems personally satisfying and growth-producing to what seems personally frustrating or destructive. The client who is experiencing some breakdown or impairment in role performance or who is violating role requirements finds himself at odds with what he expects of himself and of others, or with what others expect of him.

The caseworker will need first to learn from the client what his ideas of the role norms are (as well as what he has invested in them emotionally). He will need to match those conceptions of norms against the range of what is given acceptance or sanction in the community. He may need to help his client come to accept different norms, or to help his clients, two or more, develop compromises among their standards for themselves and for one another. But, except in instances of legal violation, the caseworker surely will not plant his feet at one spot in the continuum of behaviour and say to his client, 'There is only this one way to act as a mother, or wife, or child.' Nor, hopefully, would he commit the opposite folly and say in effect, 'Since nobody has codified exactly what a mother should or should not be and do (heaven help us if this were to happen), I will help you'—to do or to be what? to overcome discomfort in relation to what?

The fact is that social expectations and social norms are carried by everyone in a society. The role concept calls this fact to our attention and does not allow us to overlook it or forget it. It says that what we do, how we and our clients behave in any given situation, is determined not alone by our unconscious drives and needs, not only by that organisation of feelings and stances we call 'personality', but also by our conscious and half-conscious conceptions of what is called for, what is expected from us by the other(s) in a given social situation, and what we have a right to expect in return. Thus the idea implicit in role expectations places upon the caseworker several necessities: to learn from his client what he sees (his perceptions) as appropriate behaviour between the one and his role partner; to learn from him what he believes (his emotion-laden conception) each is supposed to be or do; to ask himself (the caseworker) whether the expectations invested in the role are realistic and valid (if the problem is confined to interpersonal conflict); or, when the problem is one of role-violation, a community concern, to attempt to assess it in the light of current knowledge and current social sanctions; and then to try to so influence the feelings and perceptions and expectations of the client that he modifies his expectations of himself and others with consequent better adaptation.

This last paragraph carries too heavy a burden within its narrow scope. What the caseworker must do to negotiate between role partners on their mutual expectations, or between a role violator and societal requirements, is material literally to fill a book. It is the content of casework treatment. I mention it here chiefly to take note of a comment that seems common among caseworkers today to the effect that the caseworker 'must not impose his middle-class value system upon his client'. As the comment is usually made, it is 'middle-class values' that are deplored. It seems to me it should be 'impose' that is deplored. To impose and to influence are two very different actions, with very different consequences for the individual. The fact that must be given attention is, I believe, that expectations of called-for or required behaviour are held by everyone who carries a role in relation to another. Such expectations do not differ only from class to class, from culture to culture. They may also differ from person to person in the same small family unit. Therefore, treatment of a problem of role conflict or role violation requires that the caseworker start where the client is—with the client's own definitions of what his role requires of him and ought to provide for him, then with the 'other's' ideas of his expectations of himself and his 'partner' in terms of giving and getting. Then the caseworker takes counsel with himself to recognize his own subjective biases about what people ought to be and do in given roles and to separate these, if necessary, from what current knowledge and current sanctions hold to be the norm-range, the latitude of norm. Of course there may be conflicts here. The community says, 'The unmarried mother should be punished'; the casework agency says, 'She should be understood and helped'. Only a very simple culture is free of such conflicts about role expectations. But the caseworker who starts from what his client sees and wants, and who works to bring that client into more harmonious relationship with what others require or expect, will not readily 'impose' his values, 'middle-class' or other.

Social expectations and norms and personalized expectations of give and get, effort and reward, action and response, obligation and reciprocation—all are charged with emotion. The concept of role, then, carries a fourth constant implication:

4. *Role implies that certain emotional values or sentiments tend to be injected*, in any human activities that involve given-and-taken relationships with others, either into the activities themselves or into the reciprocal relationships, or both.

'Ought', 'supposed to', 'must', 'good', 'bad', 'wise', 'stupid', 'kind', 'mean'—these are only a few of the emotionally charged value judgments that express people's feelings about how they themselves and others carry their role tasks and relationships. These value judgments and sentiments are of two major sorts: First, there are those that are generally agreed upon in a culture at large. (A mother who neglects her child is 'bad'—we deplore her; a man is 'supposed to' support his family—we are indignant when he does not.) These are cultural attitudes and feelings which come attached to role expectations generally. The second sort of sentiment and emotion in role performance is the more personalized kind—the feelings which each of us individually, within the larger culture, invests in certain roles. It is with these that the caseworker is particularly concerned.

Roles are carried and experienced by individual personalities. All or any aspects of personality may be involved in the performance of vital roles. So the role concept carries the constant reminder that feelings, attitudes, personality itself, are the *product-in-process* of old and current experiences of socially required behaviour (roles) and socially provided rewards and frustrations (role valuations). This is the recognition essential to our seeing that 'role' is not something superficial or external to the personality. Rather, from infancy, roles shape personality and are shaped in turn in an interaction process between our outer and inner realities. From the beginning, certain behaviour and reactions are 'expected' from the infant in response to the feeding, cleaning, cuddling activities prescribed for the mother. I say 'prescribed' because, although most mothers might 'just naturally' carry out these behaviours, every mother in our society knows that she is 'supposed' to do these things—that they are inherent in her role as mother of an infant. Then, if the baby violates his role—if, for example, he refuses the breast or gives no indication at the prescribed time that he recognizes, responds to, 'loves' his mother—a whole series of small ruptures begin to occur in the emotional and behavioural interaction between mother and child. All the baby books that mothers and fathers and social workers peruse with varying degrees of intensity are, in effect, codifications of the evolving roles of infant and child and of the reciprocal behaviour expectations of parents.

The concept of the id—that combination of those life-forces that push and pull us in certain ways and directions—is a concept that actually depends for its full meaning upon a recognition of the social forces and conventions that require us to move in certain ways and directions. The concept of superego is an idea of incorporated social expectations that are harmonious with or in conflict with the id's demands, or are in conflict with or harmonious with any given day's social role demands or social role rewards. The concept of ego is an idea of a negotiating function between the person's inner drives and outer demands and opportunities. Perception is the ego's first function; it is the function upon which all adaptation and negotiation depend. Ability to carry a role depends on the ego's clear perception of it. Turn this around—as one must, because an interaction process is in operation here, too—and it is plain to see that role demands may be so stressful or role definitions so ambiguous that a person's perception will be strained and dimmed and, consequently, the ego may retreat behind defence-works. We know the relation of the ego-ideal to the personality's quest for self-image and goals. How successful that quest, how realistic the ego-ideal, how appropriate the goal—all stem from the individual's past and present role experiences, his mastery or failure in the various emotion-charged roles he has carried from infancy on.

All this is to postulate the interwoven relationship between the growth and functioning of the personality and the successful or thwarted carrying of social roles. Social roles are at once the vehicles and the moulders of personality, the means through which personality is expressed and also by which it is shaped.

The implications for casework are several-fold; if important roles are charged with feeling, then our casework eyes and hands must take full account of the emotional and psychological import of failures or damage in the everyday, humdrum role problems of our clients. We need to attend more closely than has been our wont to 'the social determinants of behaviour'. We will need to understand more fully how unconscious and half-conscious drives and wants not only affect how we carry a given role but may, in turn, be affected by the gratifications or frustrations we harvest in carrying our vital roles. Consequently, our casework treatment content, focus, and goals may undergo some shifts. But this goes beyond the scope of this paper.

As the concept of social role has begun to open up for me, I have come to some fuller understanding of the meaning of 'social' in social casework and to some firmer sense of the professional identity of the social caseworker. The person's difficulty in taking on or in carrying some role—new or familiar—seems to me to be the locus for social casework's activities. This role may be that of spouse or parent or student or patient or applicant to a social agency or probationer—and the role problem-to-be-worked may shift from time to time in the life of a case. Our diagnostic concern is to understand those factors that cause or are associated with that difficulty and those that may be mobilized to cope with it. This will require our closer study and understanding of the dynamics of social interaction and of the psychology of the social.

Although the role concept is not fully developed, it promises to alert and sensitize us to these four aspects of our client's problems in social functioning; that in the role in which he is experiencing crisis or chronic trouble there are certain social activities and tasks involved; that he carries these in social interaction with others; that between him and others there are psychologically significant and socially determined norms and expectations as to the way he and the other(s) perform their tasks; that personal attitudes and vital feelings are invested in these social tasks, in the role interaction, and in the expectations of outcome. Within these as yet crudely identified parts of the role concept there lie, I believe, many further implications for casework's social understanding and action, and some new pathways open to further explorations in casework diagnosis and treatment.

READING REFERENCES

These references are selected from among the many writings on role because they offer relatively ready entry to the grasp of the role concept and its varied implications. Footnote references in the above article are not repeated in this listing.

1. Ackerman, Nathan W., ' "Social Role" and Total Personality,' *American Journal of Orthopsychiatry*, Vol. XXI (January 1951), pp. 1-17, or

2. —— 'Social Role and Personality,' in *Psychodynamics of Family Life,* chap. iv, Basic Books, New York, 1958.
3. Bernard, Jessie S., *Social Problems at Midcentury,* Dryden Press, New York, 1957.
4. Cottrell, Leonard S., Jr., 'The Adjustment of the Individual to His Age and Sex Roles,' *American Sociological Review,* Vol. VII (October 1942), pp. 617-20. Also in *Readings in Social Psychology,* ed. Theodore M. Newcomb and Eugene L. Hartley, Henry Holt & Co., New York, 1947.
5. Group for the Advancement of Psychiatry, *Integration and Conflict in Family Behaviour,* Report No. 27, New York, 1954.
6. Leighton, Alexander H., M.D., *My Name is Legion,* Basic Books, New York, 1959. See references to role in Index.
7. Linton, Ralph, 'Concepts of Role and Status,' in *Readings in Social Psychology,* ed. Theodore M. Newcomb and Eugene L. Hartley, Henry Holt & Co., New York, 1947.
8. Pollak, Otto, *Integrating Sociological and Psychoanalytic Concepts,* Russell Sage Foundation, New York, 1956, pp. 149-52.
9. Sarbin, Theodore R., 'Role Theory,' in *Handbook of Social Psychology,* ed. W. Gardner Lindzey, Vol. II, pp. 223-55, Addison-Wesley, New York, 1954.
10. Spiegel, John P., M.D., 'The Resolution of Role Conflict within the Family,' *Psychiatry: Journal for the Study of Interpersonal Processes,* Vol. XX (February 1957), pp. 1-16.
11. —— 'Some Cultural Aspects of Transference and Countertransference,' in *Individual and Familial Dynamics,* ed. Jules Masserman, Grune & Stratton, New York, 1959.

5

IDENTITY PROBLEMS, ROLE, AND CASEWORK TREATMENT*

HELEN HARRIS PERLMAN

THERE is among us today a common malaise, a sickness of spirit, a 'dis-ease' that has been recognized and delineated both by psycho-analysts and by social scientists. It has been the theme of a rising tide of literary and pictorial artistic expression in the 'theatre of the absurd', in the novel of the diffused personality, in paintings without form or structure. It has been called by many different names, but its characteristic syndrome is the loss of or lack of a sense of identity. When it is chronic, it has been named 'identity diffusion'; when it is acute, 'identity crisis'; and when it becomes an all-involving pursuit, 'the quest for identity'.

Its symptoms are these: the person is permeated by a sense of inadequacy, of confusions and self-doubt, of worthlessness, of aimlessness, of having no place in his society, no direction in which to go, no goal. He is pervaded by a melancholy sense of futility, of inability to 'take hold', or by a restless, directionless pursuit of questions for which he can find no certain answers: 'Who am I? What am I? What am I for? Where am I going? Why? What is my place and purpose?

The explanations and reasons for the prevalence and pervasiveness of this existential malaise has occupied the minds and energies of philosophers and behavioural scientists in increasing numbers over the past years. It might almost be said, if one were to be flippant, that these thinkers and investigators seem to have found their identities as unravelers of the mystery of why other people have not. At any rate, the causes that seem to be agreed upon are so complex, so involved with all the technological, automated, sped-up changes in ordinary living within a destruction-threatened, outer-space-oriented world that they all but defy being caught, halted, reversed.

* Published in *The Social Service Review*, Vol. XXXVII, No. 3, September, 1963.

Social work stands among the several helping professions that stubbornly affirm the importance of the individual human being and the importance of *inner* space—whether that inner space is within one person or within the family cluster or within a community. Social workers doggedly attend to the business of trying to free man's energies and spirit so that he can lead his life with some sense of worth and dignity and purpose. This is why we remain intent upon helping people whose life-circumstances or whose troubled spirits corrode their being.

Those people have many problems, but they are also victims of the general malaise. They often suffer from acute identity crisis or chronic identity diffusion. They do not call their problems by these names. Indeed, they usually come with problems that are more tangible, more immediate—problems of interpersonal conflicts and disturbance or of unmet needs that are usually visible and verifiable. But what they say with their eyes as they anxiously scan our faces for signs of understanding, and what they say with their sighing or apathy, by their stiffened or wilting bodies, is: 'Help me to know what to be and how to be, and what to do and how to do, and where to go and how to go, better than I can alone. Help me to find myself and my powers in a situation in which I am lost and overpowered.' Problems of identity accompany, or underlie, or are the products of, many of the other problems that beset the clients of caseworkers.

Caseworkers have been particularly aware of identity problems in adolescents. Their sensitivity to the problem in this age group derives from the fact that the literature on adolescence names it as a nuclear conflict in this life-stage[1] and from the fact that adolescents themselves often express it freely and frequently. Some identity struggle is normal for this period when, in the words of a now old-fashioned poet, the young person stands 'with reluctant feet where the brook and river meet'. The strugle becomes a 'problem' when his questions, 'Who am I? What am I? Why am I?' become so obsessive that they undermine the usual work and relationship tasks the adolescent is supposed to carry. When this happens the adolescent is often sent for casework or psychiatric help, though the problem is usually stated in terms of his symptoms—'He is delinquent', 'He is failing in school', 'He is "acting out" in rebellious or self-destructive ways'.

There are other groups of people, also typically the clients of caseworkers, in whom we have not so clearly recognized the problems of

[1] See particularly Erik Erikson, *Childhood and Society*, W. W. Norton & Co., New York, 1950.

identity diffusion or identity crisis. Unmarried mothers on ADC[1] comprise one of these groups. (To be sure, they are not often within the attention of the sophisticated caseworker. Perhaps they ought to be. By any criterion they ought to be the concern of social work.) Here is a woman, one of a mass of women, whose identity is ambiguous to the total community, then to the social worker, and basically to herself. Who and what is she? To the community she is a woman or girl who out of lust or mishap has violated the role of unmarried female. To the caseworker, who only rarely sees her, she is a relief client, who qualifies for her cheque as long as she harbours her child and has no other income. To her child she is a good or bad mother who has no husband to be his father. To herself—? One wonders what her sense of herself is—how she sees herself—what she feels herself to be and to be becoming. Maybe she never had a sense of self, of identity. Maybe her sexual vulnerability is one symptom of her lack of self-worth; of her never having felt the continuity of belonging, of being, of becoming; or of feeling her identity as a member of an outcast, socially denigrated group with nothing to gain and thus nothing to lose. No one really knows what her problem is, because thus far no one has really asked. But if professional social work will give its attention to this girl or woman and to her child, the problems of the sense of selfhood may be found to be of profound importance in what can be done to change her and her life-mode.

There are in our big cities today growing numbers of unemployed or sporadically employed men, marginal workers whose jobs are vanishing into the maw of automation. They range from the adolescent who enters the job market as a drop-out from school up through the middle-aged. They are predominantly, though not exclusively, Negro. They are sucked into the labour market by capricious industrial or agricultural needs here and there, and cast off when a market glut or a machine makes them useless. They have no skill, no steady occupation, no vocation, no reliable employment for their time and energies; their days are spent 'hanging around' in desultory, apathetic ways. They feel like nobodies, and consequently they act like nobodies—anonymous, mask-faced men with no sense of identity as workers, as husbands, as fathers, as men with goals. In the mass they constitute a serious social problem, the 'dynamite' in the city slums. Caseworkers see individuals among them now and again—the alcoholic, the young delinquent, the putative father of the newborn illegitimate child. Scratch the surface

---

[1] Aid to Dependent Children through the USA public welfare provision.

of any one of them and the sense of anomie and of missing identity will be found.

But it is not only among the masses of the economically poor or the socially outcast that one finds adults with pervasive uncertainties about themselves or about their direction. Aged men and women of all classes have problems of housing and medical care and leisure-time occupation. Threading through these problems, undermining the aged person's adaptability, is the persistent sense of identity-loss or insufficiency. Even if he had fair security about himself earlier in his life, the aged person's loss of role and of usefulness to others rouses the insistent cry within him: 'What am I? Who wants me? What am I *for*?' One further example: Family agencies and medical and psychiatric clinics are overfamiliar with persons who have become physically or psychologically isolated from their family groups or friends and who have no employment of the self either in paid work or in a vocation. Such people are literally afloat as personalities. Their sense of what they are and what they want is vague. They know their identity only in their roles as patients, as clients, as 'needers', chronic seekers of help through attachment to someone—a therapist, or something—a clinic or agency, that seems to be anchored.

Among all these varied kinds of persons are varied problems which to a greater or lesser degree are associated with the diffusion, the rootlessness and aimlessness named 'identity problems'. For all of them caseworkers are challenged to develop some ways by which to instil or enhance the person's sense of selfhood, of social value, of belonging to others, and thence of having some goal. I do not mean to imply that caseworkers have the wisdom or the means to cope with the pervasive problems of who and whither and why that are endemic in our society. That would be obviously absurd. I mean only that for the people we undertake to help we need to explore and to find every means we can by which to enhance the inner sense of worth and social adequacy.

Here I come to consideration of social role in relation to problems of identity. The causes of a person's identity problems lie in his life-history. A person's life-history is his experience of interaction with people and circumstances which, for the most part, nurtured and exercised his sense of adequacy and mastery or which mostly starved or inhibited that sense. In other words, a person's life-history consists of his role transactions from infancy onward—of what he got and what he gave, of his being rewarded or deprived, recognized or rejected, in his child-parent, sister-brother, pupil-teacher, playmate-friend, worker-employer relationships and tasks. Caught and scrutinized at any moment in his life, a person will be seen as the product of this life-experience. But he can never be caught alive and static. He is never only a product. He is always *in process*. He is in process of 'becoming', although he is a product of 'having been'. His 'becoming' may entrench what he has been. Or it may be different. This is the belief on which casework as well as every other therapeutic effort is based.

At the moment in time when a person comes to a social agency, he has one uppermost problem. It is that in some current vital life-role he is experiencing breakdown, incapacity, conflicts, or lack of gratification. This problem may have many facets and variations because at any one time a person's vital roles are several and varied, and because the personalities and partnerships involved in those roles are varied. But the uppermost problem presented to the social caseworker is that of some unmanageable or insufferable role difficulty.

I suggest that problems of identity, at the time they are seen by the caseworker (usually at a point of crisis or of acute stress), are related to role problems. They are related not only as they are explained by the person's previous and current role experiences. They are also related as they may be ameliorated, if not resolved, through a treatment focus upon helping the person find, engage himself in, and derive rewards from some vital role. Through such help his 'becoming' may be signally affected.

The experience of any one of us shows that in carrying any vital life-role a person makes a substantial investment of himself. We 'put ourselves into' such roles as wife, mother, worker, student, child; we are 'libidinally invested' in such roles. These so-called social roles are, for the human being who carries them, charged with emotion and feeling. The greater the deposit of such feeling in the role, the more wholly the personality is involved. The more wholly the person is involved, the more he as 'self' and he as 'role-carrier' merge and become one.

Under satisfactory conditions, a person is nourished by the gratifications, the drive fulfilments, the social recognitions and rewards that his role responsibilities and behaviours yield. He comes to know himself securely; he presents himself to others with confidence in his being something and somebody, whether in his family group or outside. Some of us have single roles in which we make almost a total investment of self; others invest in several important life-roles and the 'self' comes to have several dimensions. The essential point, however, is that the carrying of one or more vital roles at any stage of living is intimately related to our sense of self, to our sense of who and what we are. If this is true, it follows that one of the crucial ways by which caseworkers can help people to find themselves, to enhance their sense of identity, to increase their feelings of self-worth and purpose, is to help them to undertake and to carry some essential social role with optimal adequacy and gratification.

'If this is true—.' Because one can never know in others what one has not experienced in one's self, I suggest this test of the relation of identity to role: Look in the mirror—hard. Look deeper than that outer skin mask to which the Greeks gave the name 'persona' and from which, interestingly, we drew the words 'person' and 'personality'. Examine your identity: who and what are you?

You will be able quickly to answer that you are of a given sex, age, nationality, ethnic, and religious group, the descendant of certain people of whom you are proud or tolerant or uneasy, as the case may be, related by blood ties to a nuclear and more or less extended family group. Keep looking. You will say, 'I am I, myself, me, with certain appearances and personal characteristics, and certain qualities of body, mind, and spirit.' Have you placed yourself? Do you feel your identity whole, secure, complete?

Perhaps only a very few of us would, for only a very few of us carry that sense of internal confidence and security so certainly that we would be able to know and accept ourselves simply in our being. Most of us need to move one step further towards identifying ourselves through having some present viable connection with some other persons and/or some occupation. We seek to establish identity not simply by being and belonging in certain social categories, but by our being something and doing something in relation to other people. Most of us best recognize ourselves through what we do in our social interactions, in our relationships to people and to established life-tasks. I am myself, yes. But most of us are pushed one step beyond—to define ourselves in social terms. What we say to ourselves and to others (in other words, of course) is: 'I am a wife; I am a mother; I am a student. That is, I occupy a position and do something in one or more occupations.' And our measure of ourselves, as well as our innermost feelings of confidence and self-hood, will be affected by the social assessment and the personal satisfactions or frustrations that these roles provide.

We know ourselves most surely through our daily occupations, avocational or vocational, which link us to other people or to activities that are socially valued. In short, we know our identities in large part through our social roles.

In some older societies, perhaps still in some parts of the world, a person may know his identity through his niche in a firm, stable social structure. 'I belong to this family,' he may say, and he will find echoing into the chambers of his personality the respectful acceptance he then sees in the eyes of others. But we—and our clients—live in a society that is 'on the make', an action-oriented society. It tends to value not a person's ancestry, nor always his qualities of character, but rather the uses to which he puts himself and the consequent achievements. It is not an accident that the first question that rises in your mind when you meet a new person is 'What does he *do*?' or that the common greeting to be heard among us is 'How're you *doing*?'

One may deplore this. Indeed, Erich Fromm and others, ranging from existential philosophers to professional beatniks, have deplored the fact that man is becoming a 'functionary' in our society, that he is losing his sense of individual being. This may be happening in many of the mechanized, lock-step roles we all carry to a greater or lesser extent. But the roles or patterns of interaction with which caseworkers are concerned are those that actually hold or potentially can be endowed with emotional nurture for the personality.

The concepts of identity and role do not express the same things. The sense of identity is an accrual of largely unconscious feelings. It is felt as a sense of selfhood, of one's own powers, of the boundaries that separate the 'I' from the 'thou'. The knowledge and acceptance of one's self, with faults and frailties as well as powers and strengths, with rights of one's own and responsibilities towards others, the sense of worth and directedness—these grow out of continued experiences from babyhood onward of interaction with others and of coping more rather than less successfully with the circumstances of living. These circumstances and these people have been part and parcel of the roles we carry from infancy onward. Our sense of identity is their product.

The roles that are vital to the development and qualities of personality (and identity) are obviously not trivial ones. They are not 'acts' that we 'put on'. They are 'real' and 'earnest', our emotionally invested interactions. The concept of role, if it is to be of use to a caseworker, must be viewed and understood always in its fourfold dimensions.

1. To carry a role means to do something. So actions and behaviours are one aspect of role performance.

2. To carry a role means doing something in relation to one or more others. So interactions, transactions, and reciprocations between and among several people are a second aspect.

3. Transactions between people are shaped and governed by their

ideas, expectations, and judgments of the attitudes and behaviours of self and other. So cognition, conscious ideas, will be a third aspect of role performance.

4. Ideas, expectations, judgments of reciprocal transactions are charged with affect and shaped by drives and emotions. So drives and emotions are a fourth aspect of role performance.

When 'role' is viewed in these four dimensions, as a combination of doing, thinking, feeling, interacting, it is not hard to see how within a vital role a person's sense of selfhood and identity can be undermined or enhanced. When the requirements or the reciprocations of a given role are chiefly frustrating, the person feels undermined and under stress. When, on the other hand, a role brings satisfactions, the person feels gratification. Because our clients come to us with difficulties in role functioning, because they bring the problems that they encounter (in marriage, parenthood, employment, and so on), caseworkers are rather more perceptive of role stresses than of the potential and actual rewards to be found in adequate role performance. Thus we have not sufficiently explored the ego-enhancing, strength- and growth-promoting potentials inherent in commonplace, everyday roles.

The roles we carry may reward us and build into our sense of selfhood in a number of ways. Here, briefly, I can suggest only a few: A socially recognized role defines a position, suggests a niche that a person occupies in relation to other persons. It is a kind of anchorage. Moreover, it connects a person to at least one other, offering a sense of 'belonging'. A role expresses some function. So the role-carrier's sense of being-to-a-purpose is underpinned. Roles that are relationship-oriented promise—and yield—social recognition and support. Certain roles provide purchase power—that is, they earn or buy desired conditions or things. And roles provide certain regularities of behaviour which, then, free the person's energies for new ventures. (It goes almost without saying that the person's experience of deficiencies, distortions, or conflicts in his roles will undermine or rock his emotional well-being. There are times, too, when the carrying of a role may be at too great a cost to the personality and a person may need help to find acceptable release from excess responsibility or from his social striving at the price of psychic stress. But this is another subject.)

An exploration of the kinds of rewards with which homely, everyday roles may be invested may offer the caseworker new sources of ego-nourishment for clients. We have tended to believe that if personality changes can occur the person will function more effectively in his various roles. What I suggest here is some turnabout in our perspectives—some consideration of the possibility that modifications or changes in personality may result from the exercise of ego functions that are inevitably involved in coping with role problems, and from the feelings of gratification which may ensue.

If a client can be helped to experience some valued role more satisfyingly, if he can be freed from the undue conflicts and stresses with which he (and/or his role-partner) invests it, if he can get even the minimal reward of recognition for trying to handle himself better in his interactions with others, there will result for him some heightened sense of self as having both power and purpose. Obviously such change will not occur simply because a caseworker urges or encourages a client to 'Be a better mother' or 'Try to behave in school'. To help a person shoulder and carry a familiar role in new and more satisfying ways or take on an unfamiliar role requires every therapeutic skill that casework offers. These skills cannot be detailed here. It can only be said that they consist of the releasing and supportive sharing of the client's feeling; of the projection and correction of his perceptions; of the consideration of connections between his today and his yesterdays, his today and his tomorrow, between him (the client) and you, him, and others, between what he feels and what he does, what he does and how it affects others, what he feels and does and what he thinks about it, whether he can see it and feel it differently, and what all this has to do with what he wants for himself. This repeated exercise of the client's ego functions, supported and infused by relationship, is the essence of the casework process.

The content, that is, the subject matter under work, is the person(s) in some problematic role. The person feeling, thinking about, acting and interacting in that role, the other persons or circumstances with which he is involved, the reality requirements and potential rewards in that role—all this is content for caseworker-client considerations.

In the case example that follows, one may see illustrated a severe identity problem and the possible treatment usefulness of a focus on role:

Wade X is a seventeen-year-old Negro boy, brought by his mother to a family agency with the agreement of his probation officer. Wade has been involved in a number of delinquencies. He was with a gang when the police raided the house of a girl who claimed gang-rape; he has stolen a car for a joy ride; he has smoked 'reefers'; recently, after mounting defiance in school which culminated in his striking a teacher, he was expelled. But there is a margin for hope. Wade's mother is a responsible woman, worried about her son. Wade seems to have good

F

intelligence. Moreover, he has registered in night school classes in art and psychology because he wants 'to show' his teachers; in fact, he thinks he wants to *be* a teacher.

(In regard to the problem of identity, a seventeen-year-old Negro boy has two strikes against him to begin with. As an adolescent he is likely to be involved in all the common, but nevertheless personally poignant, problems of 'what am I, who am I, why, and where am I to go?' As a Negro he is likely to feel some alienation from the dominant groups in the community, some sense of being 'different', of being undervalued socially.[1] But this particular boy, Wade, has troubles on top of all that.) In his first interview with the family caseworker, he is glib and blame-projecting. But he is also puzzled and worried about himself. He says he sometimes wonders if he's crazy. He takes long walks but he finds himself going nowhere; sometimes he finds he is talking to himself. And his mother has told him that he does not have the right feelings about things. He wonders.

Fragments of past history begin to reveal the reasons for the boy's particular diffusion of identity. Wade's father deserted when Wade was three and his brother was five. His mother placed each child with different relatives in different cities. Wade lived with his cousins, an elderly childless couple, and while they did not adopt him he was called by their surname, Wade X. His mother visited occasionally, but Wade does not recall these visits, until one day, about four years ago, she visited him and told him that she had remarried and that he could come to live with her if he chose. Not long afterwards, Wade walked out of his foster-parents' home 'as if I was going to school' and came to live with his mother, his stepfather, and his recently arrived brother. Now at home are his stepfather and his mother, Mr and Mrs Y; his brother, who carries his own father's name, Charles Z; and our boy, Wade X. Mrs Y, his mother, speaks of her uncertainty about her current roles. She has continued to work even though married, because it did not seem right to ask her new husband to support her children. Should she quit? She finds herself suddenly a mother, but of sons who are virtually men. Her husband accepts them—but passively—and one of Wade's complaints is that his stepfather does not 'come right out' and tell him what to do.

What one sees, as this tale unfolds, is not only a childhood in which this boy experienced severe discontinuities and disconnectedness but a present in which there is no firming-up of who he belongs to or what he is. Added to the usual inner questionings in the adolescent about identity and goal, added to the usual identity struggle of the child in a

---

[1] The title of a recent book by one of the Negro's most articulate interpreters, James Baldwin, states this problem: *Nobody Knows My Name* (Dial Press, New York, 1961).

minority group, is a particular life-experience, past and present, that can only contribute to this boy's sense of vagueness, rootlessness, anomie.

Having come just this far in one interview with Wade and one with his mother, the caseworker himself is beset by problems. If he is diagnostically astute, he sees many trouble spots. 'Character disorder' is spelled out in the duration and pervasiveness of the boy's problems, in his bland affect, and in his disarming projections. There is the suggestion of a schizoid underlay coupled with some (hopeful?) neurotic threads of conflict and anxiety about himself. What does one do about personality problems that have run so long and have become so pervasive? Or about the galaxy of social problems that this boy presents?

Whatever the nature of this boy's pathology—and that nature and its severity will be revealed as beginning casework efforts to bring out his responsive behaviour—this boy has little sense of what he is, why he is here, and what he is heading for. His restless, impulsive, mindless behaviour is completely out of line with his good intelligence, certainly with his conscious goals. Neither his past nor his present anchors him. The caseworker's first goal, it seems to me, is to anchor him to his reality and then within that reality to begin to build into his sense of present being and direction. The caseworker has two major ways by which to do this. One way is through the therapeutic relationship. The other is through helping the client to focus upon some current role that concerns him, helping him to connect with it in some potentially gratifying ways.

The meaning of the words we use when we describe the casework relationship—acceptance, warmth, empathy, receptivity—is essentially this: 'I look at you as a human being. But more than that, I see and hear you, I take you in, as a particular human being: *you*. You are worth my attentiveness, my interest, my lending myself to your need.' By these demonstrated attitudes, the caseworker first affirms the applicant's unique identity.

Relationship deepens as the threads of his emotional involvement in his problems are drawn from client to caseworker. The caseworker's responsive comments, his attentive receptivity, his guidance of the talking together say, in effect: 'I accept you, and I can feel with you. You are worth my help, not only because you need it, but also because you have within you the potential for coping with what hurts or frustrates you. That "wanting" or drive in you, combined with the help I can offer you, is what makes our being together have a purpose.' By these spoken or implicit affirmations the caseworker injects into the relationship not only support but stimulation, not only acceptance but expectation. 'I take you as you are, in your *being*. But our business together is your *becoming*.' This is what the ongoing relationship conveys.

As the client begins to feel himself 'received', accepted in his own being, he comes to feel a sense of union, of at-one-ness with his caseworker. In part by conscious incorporation, in part unconsciously, he takes his caseworker's view of him into himself. The danger now is that some loss of self may occur, some blurring of the reality sense of his separate identity, which we know as one aspect of 'transference'. The caseworker's clarity about the purpose and the focus of their work together—to help the client engage himself more effectively in some present life-role—is one brake upon neurotic transference.

The client's role problem may actually be the symptom of basic personality problems, as Wade's problems are symptoms of his pervasive identity diffusion. But, while they may be seen and diagnosed whole, personality problems cannot be dealt with whole. They can best be identified, taken hold of, observed, and worked over as they show themselves in some partial and tangible aspect of today's life experience. To explore the etiology and course of Wade's many emotional and social problems would be to draw him into an endless labyrinth. Instead, I submit, the effort should be to relate to this boy as warmly and directly as he will allow and to help him tackle some part of his current life-activity. Which part? The part, the role, that feels most troubling to *him*.

For Wade, the most troubling, most tangible, most consciously desired, and most readily achieved role is that of student. In this role he sees and feels his troubles plainly; in this role he knows that his actions count, for other people will decide his future unless he undertakes some part in that decision. His success or failure in that role matters to his family, to his community, but, more, to this boy's whole unfolding image of himself. Expelled from school, without occupation, without direction, he is a nothing going nowhere and talking to himself. If, on the other hand, he wants again to undertake being a regular student, with the caseworker's help, he may be restored to some sense of doing something, going somewhere, being somebody. This sense will grow not just because he resumes this role but when, as a result of the ongoing work with the caseworker, he and the other persons involved in his studentship begin to modify their feelings and interactions with one another.

When there is identity diffusion or when the multiplicity of problems feeds into the client's internal confusion, the caseworker's focus upon some current role has particular usefulness. One value is this: Such a focus makes sense to the client. Usually this is how he has defined his problem—as trouble between himself and another and/or between himself and a set of circumstances. He can talk about these troubles because they are out in the open—or so it seems to him—in the field of interaction *between* him and his opposite. Later he may be led by the caseworker to look at what is *within* him that affects the between-him-and-other, but at the start he is likely to be focused upon himself in an interactional situation.

Wade, as far as he consciously knows, wants to resume being a student. This is where he is. Moreover, this role relates to his ideas of becoming and to his wish for anchorage.

The caseworker who understands what a meaningful role involves will know that feelings, actions, reciprocal expectations, and inter-actions must become the subject matter of the ongoing work with Wade. Moreover, the concept of focus includes not only the idea of partializing but also that of viewing in depth. Thus, if the caseworker and Wade were to focus upon his problematic role of student, such focus would involve talking over and feeling through this problem in depth and detail. What brought about the breakdown in this role? How does Wade see it, and feel it, and think about it? What does he want us to help him to do about it? What is he willing and able to invest in the solution? To be a student he must act in certain ways: how does he feel about this? Can he, with the caseworker's help, begin to see himself as acting as well as acted upon? As affecting as well as affected? Can he, supported in the relationship, get into the shoes of another—his teacher, for example—and see another's position? What difference does his being in or out of school make to his mother? Does he care? And so on.

The repeated expression and examination of self as actor and inter-actor, of self as affector as well as affected, of actions as driven by emotions, of emotions and ideas as subjects for understanding and consideration—all this would be the content of the ongoing interviews between Wade and his caseworker. Such interviews would have boundary and depth and vital reality for Wade because they would be about what he is and does and feels, now, in a clearly delineated inter-action experience. Because one or more others are always involved in any role interaction, they, at different times and for different purposes, would have to be seen by the caseworker, too—probably one or more of Wade's teachers, surely his mother, possibly his stepfather.

The permeation effect of improvement and gratification in one role upon other parts of a person's life is not hard to imagine. If Wade finds some security in being reinstated in the position of student; if his (probably awkward and tentative) efforts to control his impulses meet with some recognition by his teachers, his mother, his caseworker, perhaps even some of his peers; if he can see the steps by which he can achieve what he wants for the future instead of blindly banking on 'breaks'; if his mastery of school subjects gives him some pleasure—if these small changes can be made to happen, they will combine to build into his general sense of himself. One can expect in him a rising feeling of self-respect, a growing self-awareness, some greater sense of direction and purpose, and, underpinning all this, the sense of being worth the attention of other people. His motivation to put himself into working on his problem will be sustained when the task seems encompassable to him, if he can see and feel some small achievement. Work on a tangible role promises such boundaries and rewards.

It may happen in Wade's case—as it may with any other client—that as much as he wants to handle himself and his difficulty differently, he cannot. Try as he may, responsive within the casework interview as he may be, he repeatedly finds himself unable to carry through on his perceptions and conscious intentions. When this occurs we know that there are imperious unconscious forces at work. Then there is need for diagnostic treatment, and goal considerations, perhaps for psychiatric referral, certainly for psychiatric consultation.

A number of possible values in the caseworker's use of role have been touched on here. Particular attention has been given to an idea that one way of solidifying a person's sense of his identity is to help him gain some sense of mastery in a vital life-role. I have suggested that in carrying a socially valued role a person *does* something and therefore *is* something. The conscious sense of being something is most real when a person uses himself—his energies, his emotions, his skills—in carrying some work-tasks or love-tasks that he and others feel are important. His sense of self expands when, as in the casework interview, he is accepted and affirmed and then supported as he learns to perceive and modify his feelings and actions. His sense of worth is bulwarked as the caseworker—a person he has become attached to, a representative of society—supports the importance and value of the role he works on, as well as his efforts. His sense of aim and of future is sustained as the caseworker keeps before him his realistic goals. His rewards for trying to see himself more clearly, to share his feelings, to modify his behaviour, lie in his sense of mastery when he succeeds, in the caseworker's unflagging encouragement when he fails, and in the responses and recognition he gets from other persons involved with him. This last is of great moment, for the testing ground for selfhood and self-worth is the reflection of self we see in the eyes of the people who are part of our everyday life. The eyes of the caseworker are important mirrors; but even more important are the eyes of the people with whom we live, from whom we want love or recognition, whose eyes affirm both our person and our value.

Sometimes caseworkers feel sad because they cannot give 'enough' to make up for all the deficiencies of social and psychological nurture from which many of their adult clients suffer. Even the most intensive therapies cannot achieve this. But within the boundaries of our roles as social caseworkers and of our knowledge and skills we do have ways by which to set in motion a chain of changing attitudes and behaviours which may nourish selfhood. The sense of self, of identity, grows on the effective use of one's small powers in relation to other people and things. Our daily life-roles offer us and our clients the most tangible, immediate and accessible opportunities for testing the use of ourselves, for knowing our powers, for finding our purpose.[1] When a caseworker helps his client find himself and feel himself adequate in relation to love- and work-tasks he builds into that person's sense of personal identity and social worth.

---

[1] Erik Erikson has said these same things in these words: 'Man, to take his place in society, must acquire a "conflict free" habitual use of a dominant faculty, to be elaborated in an occupation; (and) . . . a feedback, as it were, from the immediate exercise of this occupation, from the companionship it provides . . .' ('The Problem of Ego Identity,' *Psychological Issues*, Vol. 1, No. 1) and earlier, 'The sense of ego identity, then, is the accrued confidence that one's ability to maintain inner sameness and continuity . . . is matched by the sameness and continuity of one's meaning for others.' ('Growth and Crises of the "Healthy Personality" ' in *Personality in Nature, Society and Culture*, ed. Clyde Kluckhohn, Henry A. Murray, and David M. Schneider (Alfred A. Knopf, New York, 1953), p. 216.)

6

THE FUNCTION AND USE OF RELATIONSHIP BETWEEN CLIENT AND PSYCHIATRIC SOCIAL WORKER*

ELIZABETH E. IRVINE

I WISH to consider in this paper methods used by psychiatric social workers in helping clients to overcome difficulties in relationships; in other words, to modify their attitudes and behaviour in the direction of greater mental health. My thinking is based on experience in child guidance clinics, but I believe that workers in the adult field have a proportion of clients who are capable of this kind of change, and to whom the following considerations may apply. On the other hand, I am aware that they also have many clients with whom the objective of treatment is not to produce change, but to prevent or postpone change of a deteriorative kind. Child guidance clinics also have some clients with whom it is wiser not to aim at increased insight, but to help to a more limited extent in other ways. It may be thought presumptuous to decide which clients are capable of change, but in fact I believe such decisions to be unavoidable. They may be made, not by the psychiatric social worker alone, but by a psychiatrist, a team or a whole staff group in conference, they may be tacit or explicit, they may be right or wrong, but in fact one's approach to every client, in so far as it is discriminative, implies some assessment of how much insight this person can stand, how much change is to be hoped for. These assessments may be provisional, and may be cautiously tested out during the early stages of the work, but no action can be taken without some judgment of the situation to which it should be appropriate.

If we ask ourselves why people have such difficulties in relationships as to seek specialized help, the question may seem so general as to be meaningless. We have all been trained to look for the sources of mal-

* Published in *The British Journal of Psychiatric Social Work*, Vol. II, No. 6, June 1952.

adjustment in early experience and relationships, but we also know how varied these can be. Mrs A had a drunken father, Mrs B a harsh step-mother, Mr C was the only son of an embittered and exacting widow. Mr B again may have been overprotected and infantilized. Even these statements refer only to the outstanding factor in a whole complex pattern, of which even a full social history will give only an over-simplified account. However, I believe that amidst all this variety one can trace a factor which is highly relevant to our question: the lack in early life of the kind of relationship which could remain predominantly good while permitting the integration within it of the hostile and destructive impulses which every child must experience in relation to his love-objects. Clients' accounts of their parents tend to be either too black or too white; their early family life is described either as full of conflict and hostility, or as completely free from friction or dissatisfac-tion of any kind. These idealized pictures always prove on investiga-tion to cover a great deal of hostility, which was so frightening that it had to be denied in order to preserve the loving feelings with which it could not be integrated.

Early relationships which demand the repression of all jealousy and hostility, or which are lost or broken too soon, leave the individual driven and dominated by guilt at the damage he feels he has done, anxiety at the damage he still fears to do, and fear of punishment, dis-approval and rejection. The more overpowering such negative experi-ences have been, the more they restrict adaptability, discrimination, spontaneous diversified response to others. They cause the individual to lack faith in the possibility of good spontaneous relationships which will not be destroyed by the inevitable admixture of hostility with love. They cause him to see people according to a few simple stereo-types, and to react to them in stereotyped defensive ways. He may expect to find them bad, hostile, punishing and accusing, and attempt to defend himself by dominating, placating, or avoiding any real contact. He may feel they are good, and therefore sure to disapprove of his own badness; in this case he may feel a constant need to protest his goodness, or alternatively to confess his badness, because of the guilt aroused by friendliness of which he feels unworthy. He may try to win their regard by docility and submission, which serve at the same time to protect them against his unrecognized aggressiveness. One of the defences most damaging to relationships is that of projection. A number of writers have described situations in which a mother attend-in a child guidance clinic came to see that she had projected on to a child or a husband attributes of her own which she could not bear to see in herself, and have shown how this acceptance of the problem as her own was attended with great improvements in the relationship in question. Another factor frequently found in parent-child problems is displaced restitution; a mother encountered in Israel felt a compulsion to overfeed her child because she was unable to prevent her parents from starving to death under German occupation; another may be unable to assert any authority over a child whom she identifies with a sibling of her own who died in her childhood.

If serious difficulties in relationships are always expressions of inability to tolerate and integrate ambivalent feelings, what are the implications concerning methods of helping to overcome such difficulties? There are two traditional approaches to the problem. One is to give reassurance and support, trying to increase the client's self-confidence and ability to believe in his own goodness, while at the same time trying to encourage more tolerance and understanding for others. The other is to examine the past and try to reveal its distorting effects on the present, thus facilitating the withdrawal of projections, the relinquishment of defences, the development of insight into the self and the capacity to identify with the former objects of projection. Each process is often felt to imply the necessity of a 'secure' or 'good' relationship, built up as a background for the facing of the client's problems. The nature of the 'good' relationship often remains rather ill-defined, implying mainly that the client should perceive the worker as a 'good' figure. If a client is able to believe in good figures, it is not too difficult to assume this role for him, and then to demonstrate that a good figure can be uncritical and benevolent despite the revelation of attitudes and feelings which the client has hitherto regarded as shocking and intolerable.

It has been possible in my experience to give many clients a good deal of help in this way, but there are always some who seem unable to accept one as friendly and helpful, and repulse all attempts at sympathy and understanding. There is no better way of appreciating the strength of the compulsion such clients are under to recreate the present in the image of the past than to observe the determination with which they insist that one *must* play some role of their choosing, whether it be teacher, judge, or policeman, or to notice how they struggle against entering into a relationship at all. I have been brought to realise increasingly the value of concentrating on understanding just what situation the client is trying to create, what role he is trying to force on the worker, or subtly luring her into. Since the client has difficulty in relationships, it is natural that his relationship with the worker will be disturbed, and this in some characteristic way which is an excellent guide to his problems in this field. If, for instance, a parent is overtly submissive, while trying covertly to force the worker into a dominant role, we are likely to find that problems about dominance and submission are prominent in the marital relationship and the parent-child relationship, as well as having been so in his own childhood. The client who resists or rejects the service, or defends himself against participation in the treatment process, does so in a characteristic way on account of characteristic anxieties. Something has to be done about this and the question is what. We may try to feel our way round the defences, to seek some way of demonstrating good will which will gain the client's confidence, and establish the psychiatric social worker as a real person distinct from the image he is trying to force on to her. But it may be more profitable to focus attention at this point not on the role one wants to play, but on the client and the situation he is trying to create. Here he is, creating a difficulty in relationship; what better opportunity of studying his problems at first hand and helping him to understand them? Instead of trying to establish a relationship which is free from the start from the usual difficulties, may it not be better to begin with all the usual difficulties and work from there, by recognizing and accepting them in relation to oneself, towards a relationship which will be new because these problems have been to some extent resolved in it?

I think it is useful to envisage the basic aim of our work with the client in terms of restoring his faith in the capacity of others to tolerate his aggression and hostility without hitting back savagely on the one hand, or being hurt and damaged on the other. The most direct way of achieving this end is to allow, or indeed encourage him to bring all his feelings, negative as well as positive, into the relationship with the worker, to demonstrate in one's own person the ability to accept hostility without fear, and to resist demands without anger. Often it seems not enough to do this passively. If we simply remain friendly and helpful in face of a hostile client his guilt and anxiety will tend to mount, and I believe this is the process underlying many of those cases reported closed 'for lack of parental co-operation'. If on the other hand we show that we are not unaware of his hostility, that our friendliness and lack of fear is not based on ignorance of his feelings, and that we understand something of the reason for them in terms of the present situation and perhaps also of the past, then he is apt to be considerably relieved.

This method of recognizing and verbalizing the client's feelings about the situation and the worker in an accepting and understanding way has, I think, various advantages of which the first is its value in overcoming resistances, as described above. Secondly, I think the admission of negative feelings into open expression in the worker-client relationship helps the client better than anything else to realize that they are less harmful than he supposed, and will reduce the guilt and anxiety attached to such feelings, and the need to project and deny them, more effectually than anything else. I think the 'good' worker-client relationship, in which only positive feelings can be acknowledged, involves a danger of perpetuating a false belief in ideal and frictionless relationships, and so constituting by contrast a reproach to the client's friends and relations. When the relationship is kept 'good' in this sense there seems to be a danger that the client's other relationships may be overloaded with hostilities engendered, but not expressed or recognized, in the treatment situation. On the other hand, when hostile feeling can be accepted in the worker-client relationship, I think this relationship can then serve to some extent as a lightning conductor in respect of the outside relationships.

A striking example of this occurred with a very unhappy woman who complained that nobody understood her, nobody would let her talk about her sufferings in concentration camps, and yet became increasingly anxious and unwilling when encouraged to use the interviews in this way. Eventually she explained her conflict by telling a parable of a man who had committed a crime, and was advised to ease himself of the secret by whispering it to a tree; he did so, and felt greatly relieved, but the tree died. The interesting thing was that her child had already been much less anxious and defiant for some weeks, apparently because the pressure on her was relieved by the diversion of some of the mother's hostile wishes and anxieties on to the worker. I feel it is valuable in such a case to show understanding of the feeling expressed by some such phrase as 'You seem to feel it wouldn't be safe for me to hear your experiences?'; otherwise the anxiety can lead to complete blocking or even withdrawal. Some workers might also take up the theme of the crime at that point, while others might prefer to wait for further clarification and more direct expression before dealing with it.

The form of comment or interpretation is very important, and difficult to illustrate in the space available. For instance, one may feel that the client's late arrival is an indication of resistance which one would like to 'take up'. But this phrase could cover forms of comment which might increase the resistance, as well as forms which may reduce it. If one merely says 'You are a bit late today. Perhaps you didn't want to come?' this may be felt as an accusation or reproach, and the interpretation denied, even if correct. It may be more helpful not actually to mention the lateness but to say, 'I wonder if it wasn't so easy to come today?' or 'I wonder if anything we talked about last week has been bothering you?' On the other hand, if the client is obviously anxious or guilty about his lateness it may bring him more relief to discuss it openly. I think the criterion is to put oneself in the client's place, and to remember that the function of such an interpretation is not simply to point out something, but to make it easier for the client to admit. A tentative form of interpretation is also useful. It not only guards against forcing a mistaken interpretation on the client, but helps to avoid slipping into a situation in which the worker is the authority who knows best; it implies instead that the client is recognized as a person who is trying to work out his problems with the help of the worker.

In discussing this self-conscious use of the worker-client relationship and the emotional situation in the interview, questions often arise as to whether psychiatric social workers can safely and properly use 'the transference', or in fact whether anybody but an analyst should do so. I think there are several ambiguities involved in the use of this term. It was originally coined by Freud to connote the way in which analytic patients react to the analyst with the same intense positive and negative feelings which they originally entertained for their primary love-objects. It then became evident that, like all the other mechanisms observed in analysis and in neurosis, this was a special case of a process which also occurs in normal people and in ordinary social relationships; namely, the distortion which people tend to impose on inter-personal situations in view of assumptions, expectations and prejudices unconsciously derived from past experience. If this is accepted, it becomes evident that such factors must also exist in a casework situation. These emotional situations are not created by our awareness, they existed before we knew the client, they intrude into our relationship with him or remain latent in it whether we recognize them or not. However, we do not, like the analyst, deliberately encourage a regressive reliving of very early experiences. Nor do we try to intensify the relationship to such a point that it becomes, as in analysis, the most important thing, for the time being, in the patient's life.

It has perhaps created some confusion in this country that the term transference has come to be used not only in the narrow specialized sense defined above (and now distinguished by the term 'transference neurosis') but also in a broader sense which denotes the total emotional situation between worker and client, and which includes, but is not exhausted by, these emotional residues. It is perhaps in this broader sense that a psychiatric social worker can be said to 'use the trans-ference (if one prefers to use the term). It has been a matter of some uncertainty whether the relationship and the emotional situation can be used in the way I have been trying to indicate by general case-workers, or indeed by any but analysed psychiatric social workers. I think the answer is that, while personal analysis is required for work at deeper levels (and I still mean levels far short of the deepest) I hope for a time when all caseworkers will have sufficient psychological training and insight to be able at least to recognize and accept the uppermost levels of the client's feelings, and to discuss them with him where appropriate. Many caseworkers at present, when confronted with a dependent client, feel themselves to be in a dilemma between fitting into his pattern by making plans for him to carry out, on the one hand, or saying to him, on the other: 'Well, you know, this is your problem and you have to make the decision.' I would like to see them able to say, for instance: 'I wonder why you feel you can't do anything with-out me?'

7

THE FUNCTION AND USE OF RELATIONSHIP IN PSYCHIATRIC SOCIAL WORK*

E. M. GOLDBERG

THERE is increasing recognition that the deliberate use of the relationship between client and social worker can be of great therapeutic value in all forms of personal service. More knowledge is needed however about the nature of this therapeutic relationship under varying conditions. For example, settings, types of clients and treatment goals differ considerably and thus call for a differentiated use of therapeutic tools, one of which is the client-worker relationship.

In the field of child guidance the social worker functions in a clinical setting, and as a rule clients are seen regularly for a fixed time in the impersonal intimacy of the consulting room. Many clients, though disturbed, are aware of their need for psychological help and capable of some degree of insight and change. This treatment situation offers good opportunities for intensive therapy in which use can be made of the client-worker relationship.[1] Here we try to help our clients to unburden themselves and to see how they have carried the past into the present; we also hope to recognize and articulate in the 'here and now' of the treatment relationship some of the clients' problems in other relationships which usually centre round the feelings of love and hate. We try to help our clients to become aware not only of their positive feelings for us but also of their defences and unresolved hostilities towards us. We hope to demonstrate that, although we know about some of their bad, hostile feelings, we remain unharmed by them and friendly towards our clients. This experience, often a new and creative one, may

* A revised version of a paper originally published in *The British Journal of Psychiatric Social Work*, London, No. 8, Nov. 1953.
[1] E. E. Irvine, 'The Function and Use of Relationship between Client and Psychiatric Social Worker,' *British Journal of Psychiatric Social Work*, No. 6, p. 21, June 1952. (In this present book, p. 88.) H. M. Bree, ditto, p. 27.

help to lessen their fears of potential destructiveness. Whereas formerly we consciously or unconsciously tried to provoke in our clients love or positive feelings for us, by being friendly figures who brought out 'the good' in them, we are now trying to see also the hidden expression of their negative feelings towards us and to attempt to work through them. We do this because it is likely that these negative hostile feelings form the basis of their disturbed interpersonal relationships.

Most of us find this endeavour to bring hostile and negative feelings out into the open very difficult indeed, since we prefer to be loved rather than hated and find work with our positive, co-operative patients much more reassuring and rewarding. Yet we accept the existence of ambivalence both in theory and in our own life experience. It is thus reasonable to suppose, for example, that under the surface of the good, confiding mother we are interviewing, there are smouldering also ideas and feelings such as these: 'I wonder what she would do if she knew how impossible I am, how irritating I find her at times. She would probably send me away. No, I must never let her see my doubts about treatment; yet I wish she would give me more attention. She seems to have cut the hour short recently—I dare say she isn't really interested in me at all. Still, I must not let her down, she has been so understanding, she has helped me to unravel so much that was twisted and hopeless. Yet how do I know whether I can trust her, for if she knew how bad I really am . . .' and so on. If we could bring these feelings to the surface, the fear of the punishing parent, the doubts about being loved, the fear of destroying the loved object, and if we could then trace them to where they belong way back in childhood and not to us as real persons at all, this would enhance the therapeutic value of our work. We are not artificially creating this complex kind of relationship. The ingredients—both positive and negative—have always been there; but we are now ready to open our eyes to the hidden negative aspects.

We have known all along that whenever two people meet a relationship is created, and that these two people do something to each other, consciously and unconsciously. If a person is in need and turns to another one for help, the helper takes on a symbolic role far beyond his actual significance as a real person. When we become patients we often feel in a dependent childhood situation, and it is natural that we should transfer to the therapist all kinds of attitudes that rightly belong to our childhood. This simple truth became vivid to me the other day when for the first time in my life I attended a hospital out-patient department as a patient and went through the process of a fairly complicated examination. The childish fears and resentments that crowded in on me were a most telling lesson which I shall never forget. It was painful, for example, to listen to the radiographers asking each other's advice about the adjustment of the apparatus and ignoring me as a person. I felt they ought to know, be completely sure and competent, and give their exclusive attention to me: 'Parents ought to know and ought to care.' Thus, whether we like it or not, our patients tend to invest us with roles and attitudes far beyond the scope of the reality situation. It seems desirable to explore the meaning of these roles and use this stage, which is there ready made for us, to understand the patient's and our part in the drama. However, as I hinted before, our eyes are understandably more open to the dependent roles our patients play which put us into the position of good wise parents; they are less open to the signs of resistive and attacking roles, which put us in the position of unloving and persecuting parents.

The mother of a boy who was stealing and displaying nervous mannerisms was depressed and rather hopeless in her attitude, and revealed fairly soon in her treatment that she never felt loved by the maternal grandmother who was much too busy being a publican's wife. The mother was the youngest girl in the family and she had always felt imposed upon by her elders. There were many indications that she considered herself worthless, and she took it for granted that nobody cared for her very much. Her husband had lost interest in her; she was fat and unprepossessing in her looks. Early in treatment it was possible to use her relationship with the clinic by interpreting to her her puzzlement at this new experience of being wanted and respected and taken seriously. This mother, however, could not bring herself to believe in the goodness of the psychiatric social worker and the situation she presented. In the past she had avoided relationships for fear of disappointment. She always had to give people things and could not deny her children anything. There were many examples of her giving presents to people which they did not really need and of her own inability to accept presents. It seemed likely that in this way she was trying to gain love and to make reparation for her own destructiveness. The situation in the clinic, as she revealed later, was intolerable for her because she could not *do* anything, give anything in return, but had to receive. It was as yet impossible for her to believe that she could be loved for herself.

After a fairly positive beginning with the psychiatric social worker, when she unburdened herself about her early life, the unloving maternal grandmother, and the imposing sisters, there was a kind of dissatisfaction. The social worker then brought out the mother's negative feelings, namely, that the worker thought they were not really getting anywhere.

G

This led to a discussion of the mother's fear of imposing herself and need to deprive herself, and her consequent lack of faith in a good 'giving' situation. Her feelings of worthlessness were another indication that she thought of herself as a bad person, and it was put to her that her running away from relationships and her disinclination to talk at the clinic were defences against revealing her feelings of badness. It gradually transpired that the mother's youngest sibling, whose name she had completely forgotten, died when the mother was about three. She made a significant remark in this connection which revealed the burden of her guilt, 'at any rate I have not committed murder', and again she talked about how sensitive she was to other people's feelings and how she always gave up in face of difficulties. She wanted to know whether the social worker also gave up in face of difficulty. This was probably an indirect way of finding out whether the social worker rejected her too, for a little later on she referred to herself as a dustbin, something, as the social worker pointed out, which contains things people don't want. In one of the following sessions the mother saw some flowers on the social worker's desk and her remark was, 'someone must have been robbing your garden. I think I must have been a robber in my previous existence.' Here we hear expressed apparently casually, in response to an ordinary situation, the mother's secret fear of her feelings of badness, of her greedy thirst for love, of having robbed, presumably, her parents for it. And we now understand why she finds it so difficult to discuss her son's stealing. Her resistance to coming, the apparent uselessness of the interviews, her fears of revealing herself became more and more open and were recognized and verbalized by the psychiatric social worker who remained friendly and accepting. In the next interview the mother again referred to 'that murder I did which makes me feel so bad' and again expressed her feelings of hopelessness, how she could not be helped and never ought to ask for help.

Finally, the mother sat silent for almost an hour's session, the social worker sitting with her and only occasionally breaking the silence by commenting that the mother was probably afraid of what the social worker might see if she spoke. At the same time the social worker indicated that she accepted the mother with her resistance and her silence, and that the hour was still hers whatever the mother chose to do in it. After that the mother twice refused to come up to the social worker's room, preferring to sit in the waiting-room knitting and writing letters. Again this was accepted and the social worker indicated that she would be in her room, that the hour still belonged to the mother and that she would not see anyone else. After this severe testing out period the mother became increasingly more friendly and though she was still unable to believe in the goodness of the clinic she was able for the first time to discuss her deep feelings of despair over her husband's rejection, the compensations she found in her successful work as a shop assistant, and her guilt over being away from her family so much.

Here then we see a depressed woman who is unable to believe in a good figure, and whose co-operation could only be won by working through her negative feelings about her parents, her siblings, the world in general and the clinic and the psychiatric social worker in particular. It was possible to show her that the psychiatric social worker recognized these feelings and their origin, but that she was able to tolerate this hostility without retaliation whilst maintaining faith in the good part of the mother. Now that the mother is sure that the social worker knows about the bad things in her and still believes in the good part of her, she is able to gather up fresh courage to discuss her most distressing relationship, that to her husband. It seems as though the path has been cleared, but there is a long way to go yet. If, on the other hand, the social worker had taken the mother's remarks about not wanting to bother her at face value and had administered reassurance, this would have perpetuated the mother's evasiveness and would have helped to reinforce her defences. The core of the woman's problems in all relationships, namely her robbing and murdering fantasies, her feelings of worthlessness and badness and her resultant withdrawal would never have been touched at all.

This technique of bringing to light hidden hostility in a relationship seems sound common sense in the light of our own significant relationships. We often start a relationship by attempting to hide our shortcomings at all costs, but there is ever present the lingering fear that we may give ourselves away, and this anxious pretence may build up an imperceptible barrier. On the other hand, we all know the tremendous relief that comes when the significant person has seen the worst in us and yet emerges undamaged and still loving and friendly to us.

The second example demonstrates a similar point. The mother of a child with a psychosomatic complaint, a deeply disturbed woman, blamed herself for the child's troubles, never tiring of showing the psychiatric social worker how her behaviour had caused most of the difficulties in the child. Yet she was unable to accept her position as a patient. There were continual difficulties about cancelling appointments. When the mother did attend she would listen for the child coming out of the psychiatrist's room, anxious to get away at the earliest possible moment. This woman, like the other one, seemed quite unable to believe in the clinic's ability to help her.

After several sessions in which a great deal of significant history had emerged and the pattern of the present situation had become evident, it was suggested to the mother that she felt the clinic was no good and was unable to help, just as no one before had ever been able to help, for example the doctors at various hospitals. This brought denial. However, a story followed of how one doctor had told her that she was seeing things out of proportion, when she revealed to him her great concern over the child's growth of hair over her lips, which is in fact hardly visible. (This anxiety related to the mother's dreams and phantasies of having given birth to a hairy monster. These phantasies had been interpreted by the psychiatric social worker as representing her fears of her own badness and its consequences.) It was clear that the unhelpful doctor was identified with the psychiatric social worker who did not appreciate the mother's anxiety. This was indicated to the mother and a discussion ensued about how the psychiatric social worker did under-stand her underlying fears about the hairy monster and her own feelings of badness which these represented. They were then able to talk about how the mother had been trying to make good by giving the child as much good food as possible, and how painful the child's constant rejec-tion of her food had been. With more feeling than ever before, the mother said, '—painful, you have no idea what it feels like'. This remark opened up new possibilities of discussing her aggressive punish-ing feelings as a retaliating move. The picture thus emerged of a 'bad' mother giving birth to a hairy monster, producing bad food that was rejected, and who also felt responsible for the child's illness. No wonder that she felt that she was destroying whatever she touched, and it is clear that no amount of reassurance would have got around this funda-mental problem. It was interesting to observe that during the session in which these bad, destructive feelings were related to the psychiatric social worker and the clinic and discussed freely, the mother stayed eagerly to the end of the session without listening for the child.

How do we use relationships in other spheres of psychiatric social work such as the mental hospital, the out-patient clinic, or the com-munity field? It has been said that work in these settings is often sub-ordinated to the demands of a pressing reality situation and that our patients may not be capable of insight.[1] The important point was made

[1] M. H. Bree, op. cit.
H. E. Howarth. Paper delivered at a General Meeting of the Association of Psychiatric Social Workers, London, 1951.

that we must not get lost in our clients' internal problems but that our functions are distributed over a wide field ranging from practical services to relationship problems and that it is necessary to keep a balance between the 'outer' and 'inner' needs of our clients. The conditions of work in a mental hospital, or in an out-patient department, are often very different from the clinical setting just described. We may do more home visiting, which gives a different slant to our relationship with the client. At times we hardly have a quiet office in which to interview. We often have to take immediate action dictated by dire emergencies. Is it true that because of this we are less important to the patients we are trying to help? Is it not possible that, if we but care to look, the transference is there in many guises?

As previous writers have mentioned, behind the pressing reality problem there often lurks an equally important internal problem. Some might suggest that it is the psychiatrist's role to deal with the inner world of the patient, whereas we deal with his outer world. For example, a patient might be treated for his neurosis by the psychiatrist, who would be concerned with his intra-psychic conflicts, while the psychiatric social worker might deal with his social problems by helping him find a job. I wonder whether the patient can be split up in this way. We may fulfil a different role from that of the psychiatrist in relation to the patient. But I am inclined to think that, if we work with a patient, we have to accept that the whole of him is involved in the relationship with us, however much we may have to limit our function. It is therefore still important to understand our relationship with him and this in no way excludes the possibility of doing a great many chores.[1]

The performance of these chores is then not only dictated by the demands of the reality situation, but also takes into account the patient's inner problems and the use he is making of his relationship with us. The 'demands of the reality situation' often provide a wonderful umbrella under which we can hide. We may suddenly detect, for example, that a patient has us running around in circles after each emergency, and so is successfully controlling the relationship, or we might slave away getting a divorce sorted out only to find that deep down the patient has no wish to leave his spouse. In keeping us busy the patient has successfully warded off the evil hour when the real, basic situation will come to light and have to be discussed.

Awareness of the meaning of our relationship and our activities with the patient does not lead us to ignore his housing needs and his vocational problems. However, we may scrutinize more carefully in the first

[1] M. H. Bree, op. cit.

place what these activities mean to us. For example: Do we like getting things done? Do we enjoy tidying up an involved situation success-fully, almost irrespective of the patient's needs? Next, we may try to understand what these activities mean to the patient in relation to us. Does he attempt to control the situation by keeping us busy? Does he look to us as a powerful support? Does he need to test us to see how far he can go? We may then endeavour to make him aware of the way in which he is using us and perhaps other significant people in his environment. This does not mean that we hand the problem back to him. Having gained some insight into his real needs, both 'outer' and 'inner', we shall be able to relate our efforts to them rather than merely to the apparent demands of the reality situation.

Here we may remember the almost insatiable demands some psycho-paths make on us, the way they turn up at 2 p.m. on a Saturday after-noon without money or lodgings, and our well-meaning attempts to give them a good experience and offer them a 'never-exhausted breast'. Yet is it not likely that, just as the baby feels more guilty the greedier he becomes, so will our childish psychopath feel beneath his demanding behaviour? Can we perhaps help him more by talking with him about the way he is behaving with us and what the possible reasons may be for his need to behave in this particular manner? This is in fact more difficult than rushing around raising loans and finding lodgings and jobs. I expect that the latter fulfils deep reparative needs in us, whereas the former smacks of being a denying and frustrating parent who will have to face in due course the frustration and aggression he provokes in the child-patient.

The three following cases illustrate some of the problems posed by our patients. The first case is from a child guidance clinic but might also occur in any adult out-patient clinic. Here the psychiatric social worker worked with the mother of an eight-year-old girl who was suffering from temper trantrums and tics, and who probably engaged in a good deal of homosexual play with her sister; she also had a chronic vaginal inflammation. The girl was below average in intelligence. The mother, a drab, fairly simple woman, was worn down by failure. She had married a man, possibly a defective, who was exceedingly dirty in his habits. She had hoped to reform him but failed. There were two defective children. She soon revealed that the girl was not her husband's child. The mother was full of disgust and negative feelings about her husband and was applying for a separation during the early stages of clinic treat-ment. However, her fear of the court case became evident soon and also her guilt lest he might 'go to the bad' completely. It seemed as though she needed this dirty, useless husband as a safeguard against something worse, namely her own dirty sexuality. When the worker tentatively indicated to her, in a very simple way, that his dirt was 'outside' but hers 'inside', she came out with the story of her own lack of love in childhood, her misdemeanours, her period in an approved school, and finally the culmination of it all in her incestuous intercourse with her father.

Many social workers had been involved in the case before, helping the mother on the basis of the bad external situation. They had made attempts to 'clean the father up' and to arrange for the separation of the parents. But they had not seen the hidden inner conflict of the mother's dirt and guilt and her need to hang on to her husband as both a means of reparation and a means of punishing herself. So far, in treatment, this mother had been developing a very positive relationship to the psychiatric social worker as someone who could tolerate the dirt and misery and failure in her life. She had blossomed forth into a 'perm' and looked a different woman. However, the time would come when she would have to face the fact that the psychiatric social worker could not be a permanent loved parent who would expiate her from her sins, and that in the relationship with the social worker she would have to tackle her inner problem of rejection and destructive, guilty sexuality. The psychiatric social worker had the immensely delicate task of never losing sight of both the grim reality situation, with its daily misery and frustration, and the inner problems which chained this woman to the outer reality.

The second case, taken from mental hospital work, illustrates a different kind of dilemma, which is common, between internal and external need. It concerns a youngish couple; the wife was suffering from torticollis, was very much disabled and grossly unstable; the husband was a rather inadequate man with a cleft palate, who was consciously trying to build with his wife and small son, aged eight, the home he had never had in his deprived childhood. It became clear that the child was suffering through being with two such severely physically and emotionally handicapped parents and that he needed a more stable normal environment. The internal needs of the father clearly necessitated leaving the family intact, but the reality of the situation meant suffering and possible later emotional disturbance for the child.

Here again the psychiatric social worker had the role of interpreting and relating the internal to the external needs. She had the courage to leave the child for a time in these unsuitable surroundings, while the parents were building up a relationship with her and were learning to trust her. With great skill she gradually led the father to recognize that although his own childhood had been unhappy because of parental rejection and subsequent suffering at a boarding school, his sending his son in turn to a boarding school could become a helpful and constructive act. The psychiatric social worker did not reassure or persuade. She was able to show the father in her relationship with him that she understood his underlying fears and his guilt, and she helped him to face these problems so that he could see reality as it was, rather than in terms of his own childish suffering. Once this was achieved the father took a leading part in making all the arrangements. There was none of the hostile acquiescence with which some of our clients allow us to make the practical arrangements for them to which they have been persuaded without first resolving the underlying conflicts.

The third example is unusual, but shows vividly what difficult reality situations we can tackle provided we assess the situation correctly and are aware what roles we and the patient play in it. This young man of twenty-five was an irresponsible alcoholic, the son of weak, indulgent parents who had never been able to deny him anything. In hospital he was treated with a drug and it was essential that he should continue to take it regularly outside. The psychiatrist felt that this young man had never had sufficient guidance from his parents and the psychiatric social worker was assigned the role of an educator and firm father substitute. He took on this job with a full awareness of the kind of relationship it involved; he supervised the patient carefully, not letting him get away with any of his irresponsible excuses. When the patient did not keep appointments he followed him up insistently, but most important he tried to make sure that he was taking the drug. When it became apparent that he had not taken it, the psychiatric social worker visited. He was not put off by the patient's lies, which were designed to prevent his entry, and finally startled the family by doing something which had never happened in that home before: he took a consistent line of action and saw it through. He asked the patient to fetch a glass of water and insisted that he took a tablet there and then. This was a shattering experience for father and son alike. For the first time the patient was not able to get away with excuses and had met a father figure who could give orders, insist that he be obeyed and remain friendly. The second crucial experience in this relationship was when the patient had been drinking again and his girl friend had given him up. The patient came to see the social worker and implored him to put in a good word with his fiancée. The psychiatric social worker refused and discussed with him why he could not do it. This was another startling and new experience: a father figure who could resist demands and yet remain friendly and helpful. This indeed proved to be the turning point in the case. The young man set out to take action himself and win his fiancée back by steady behaviour.

In this case we can see clearly the demands of the reality situation, namely to stop this man drinking, and the underlying problem of the impulsive, greedy infant who had never been denied anything and who attempted to manipulate the psychiatric social worker accordingly. The social worker refused to play the patient's game, took drastic and vigorous action but kept his eye on both the outer and inner reality. He did not merely manipulate the situation from the outside; he played an active role in the dynamic relationship, interpreting to the patient continuously what the patient was doing, why he was doing it and why he, the psychiatric social worker, took the steps he did. In their relationship he gave this patient experiences he had previously lacked, those of tolerating control and frustration. These experiences became growing points towards more mature behaviour.

We conclude that even in the busy to and fro of complex external social problems we need to keep an eye on the underlying inner forces in the personalities of our clients which interact with their social problems, and on the relationship which involves us with the patient. We have also seen that insight into the nature of the relationship and the roles it assigns to patient and worker is not synonymous with passivity on the worker's part and withdrawal into the consulting room.

I would like to add a few questions about the use of relationship in the supportive type of treatment, which needs a certain amount of scrutiny. A well-known medical superintendent used to ask smilingly: 'Supporting what? The neurosis, I suppose?' What exactly do we mean by 'supportive treatment?' There is our role of supporting partially-recovered psychotics or defectives in the community, providing the kind of bridge between the hospital and the community that these patients so often need. Here we function rather like a guardian or teacher trying to develop and strengthen emotional and social skills or intellectual aptitudes in our clients within the framework of a steady dependable relationship.

There are other types of cases which worry me: the people who land on us whenever they are in trouble, the people who are continually entangled in some problem or other. We may help to sort their problems out, they feel relieved and are able to carry on for another month or two. We may know these patients over a number of years. Are we really helping them, or are we choosing the line of least resistance, acquiescing in their dependence and avoiding the painful fact that there are clients and problems that we are unable to tackle? Does this procedure not remind one very much of the coloured bottle and the placebo in medicine? Even a few such cases can be a considerable millstone around our necks, taking up time which we might spend more profitably. It may occasionally be helpful to ask: Why is this patient coming to me? What does he get out of the relationship? What do I get out of it? Have I been able to help him? Do I know what his basic problems are? The answers to these questions may occasionally confirm the suspicions of the medical superintendent just quoted.

Finally, I want to touch on a comparatively new field in psychiatric social work where the relationship turns out to be just as important a tool as in any other, namely the field of research. Here one is often in a relationship with someone who is not in need of help and therefore may not be willing to reveal painful and emotionally charged experiences. He has no symptoms which may act as a signpost to possible significant childhood situations. He is just an ordinary stranger and the roles are reversed: the psychiatric social worker needs help from him. Yet she would like to find out much the same things as she does about patients: how he gets on with his wife, what he feels about his children, his job, his parents. What is she to do?

The way towards obtaining the information seems to me to use the only tool at our disposal, the relationship, and make it a living, meaningful experience for the subjects. Whatever topic they bring up we will listen with the same kind of tolerance and double attention to the words and the music behind them as we do in our therapeutic work. We shall try to assess the roles the subject assumes in the relationship and the roles he assigns to us. When the opportunity arises we may venture to make a comment, an 'interpretation' which shows that we understand what they are trying to tell us, or possibly even more: that we can help them put together puzzling feelings and experiences which they have not been able to understand or to link before. In this way one may be able to establish the give and take of a therapeutic relationship which helps to bring to light significant emotional material. However, we may have to exercise more restraint than in therapeutic work not to disturb any equilibrium our subject may have established, even though this may constitute a neurotic kind of adjustment. There is no space here[1] to discuss the tenuousness of such a relationship, where both positive and

---

[1] A paper by the writer discussing these problems in greater detail entitled 'Experiences with Families of Young Men with Duodenal Ulcer and "Normal" Control Families,' appeared in *The British Journal of Medical Psychology*, Vol. XXVI, Parts 3 and 4, 1953.

negative attitudes have to be kept within certain limits because one can neither undertake a long-term contact nor, in the cause of science, can one risk breaking off the relationship if this can possibly be avoided.

In conclusion: the initial suggestion that the relationship between the psychiatric social worker and the client is central to all psychiatric social work has been borne out by an examination of some of our activities. I have tried to indicate by various case examples how the use of relationship needs to be carefully adjusted to the setting in which we work, to the type of client and problem we deal with, and the aims we are pursuing.

While psychoanalysis has provided a theory for understanding the nature and use of relationship, the casework situation is sufficiently different from the analytic one to warrant separate study. Questions that need to be asked are: In what way does the transference situation differ in casework from that in analytic work and what factors determine its limits? How do we achieve the balance in treatment between the outer and inner needs of the case which is probably the crucial difference between our approach and the psychotherapeutic one? How do we gain sufficient self-knowledge (acknowledging the impracticability of full analysis for all of us) to cope with our own biases and blind spots in relationship, so that we can see the needs of our clients distorted as little as possible by our own needs for love and approval on the one hand, and for power on the other? These questions urgently clamour for answers: they are well within reach of being explored seriously and systematically.

8

TRANSFERENCE AND REALITY IN THE CASEWORK RELATIONSHIP[*]

ELIZABETH E. IRVINE

DURING the celebrations of the birth of Sigmund Freud, lectures were given in London exploring the contribution of his discoveries to such varied fields of human knowledge as philosophy, education, child care, social problems in industry and the understanding of art. Are we ready and able to give an account of that which our own profession of social casework has extracted from this inexhaustible mine? To some extent I think we are. It has not been easy to think clearly on this topic, largely because our vision has been obscured by the emotional significance of a number of the questions involved. For instance, was casework psychotherapy? If so, it was often assumed, it must be an inferior form of psychotherapy; and it was often concluded that for this reason it was preferable to think of it as something different, whether we could define the difference clearly or not. Clarity could only come as this cloud of feeling subsided, and a good deal of doubt and confusion still exists. Thus at a refresher course of the Association of Psychiatric Social Workers we were told by a psychoanalyst[1] that casework and psychotherapy are for him indistinguishable; while a psychiatric social worker contributed a paper on the distinction between casework and psychotherapy.[2] I have come to the conclusion that this is largely a semantic problem (once it has ceased to be an emotional problem) based on the unexamined assumption that the term psychotherapy and the term casework each refers to a unitary entity—or in other words that each time anyone uses one of these terms he is talking about the same thing, so that anyone else knows exactly what he means. In Dr Sutherland's paper referred to above he cuts very cleanly through this Gordian

[*] Published in *The British Journal of Psychiatric Social Work*, Vol. III, No. 4, 1956.

[1] J. D. Sutherland, 'Psychotherapy and Social Work,' *The Boundaries of Casework*, London, Association of Psychiatric Social Workers, 1956.
[2] A. B. Lloyd Davies, 'Psychotherapy and Social Work,' ibid.

knot: 'Psychotherapy ... can mean almost anything in regard to its aims and methods. All kinds of people can help the psychologically disturbed in all kinds of ways. Many people even have a remarkable intuitive understanding of unconscious motives and can help through this understanding. I should like to restrict psychotherapy, however, to any psychological treatment whose aim is to permit the individual to gain insight into the nature and origins of certain unrecognized parts of himself, when such treatment is based on theoretical principles which are formulated and ~~into~~ which can therefore be subjected to at least some checks in regard to their validity.'[1]

I think this formulation gives us a framework within which we can see that casework, no less than psychotherapy, is a term which in common use represents a variety of different things, and that if we restrict the use of the term psychotherapy as Dr Sutherland suggests there is a considerable overlap between the two; in fact that some forms of casework are psychotherapy in Dr Sutherland's sense and some are not. Even among psychiatric social workers, some are much more concerned with developing insight in his sense than others, some work on the basis of a body of formulated principles, and some mainly on the basis of intuitive understanding. This latter group tend to be insufficiently represented in professional discussions, and perhaps insufficiently regarded, because they are almost by definition less able to express their methods of helping in words. If I do not explicitly include their work in the survey I am about to attempt, this is because I lack knowledge and understanding of it, not through lack of respect; and it may be that some of my formulations will in fact be found to apply to some of these ways of helping.

In taking stock of our debt to Freud, we should differentiate clearly between the two elements of his bequest to the world, both indifferently known as 'psychoanalysis'; I refer to the body of psychodynamic theory on the one hand and to the therapeutic method on the other. As regards the theory, we can now see how much of what appeared at first so revolutionary and shocking had been contained in the mythological and artistic tradition of our own and other civilizations; Freud himself paid generous tribute to his forerunners, the great poets and dramatists of the world. What shocked us or our parents so deeply was his rediscovery and restatement in the scientific form, which alone confers respect for knowledge in our time, of insights which had been tolerable only in mythological form; his increasingly well-documented insistence that the curse of Oedipus lay heavy on us all, on the psychological

[1] ibid.

reality of such poetic statements as that 'we are all members of one another' and that if we ask for whom the bell tolls we shall find it tolls for us. It is true that we were also shocked by the explosion of a modern myth concerning the innocence of childhood, and by the revelation that the fairy tales which some banish from the modern nursery are in fact very graphic accounts of the inner world of the child.

In short, the knowledge of the human heart which was contained in fairy tale and saga, in Norse myth and Greek tragedy, in the Bible and in the work of Shakespeare, Ibsen and others was confirmed, elaborated, extended, systematized and brought home not only to the patient, but also to the common reader. Gradually this great body of systematized knowledge imposed itself, and established its indispensable importance for the understanding of human personality, behaviour and interaction, and of the therapeutic processes by which these can be changed. Whether in its classical form or in various derived or modified forms, it became the basis for psychotherapy in Dr Sutherland's sense, it was gradually incorporated in the training of psychiatric social workers, and eventually, in the USA, of caseworkers in general. Here, this last stage is only just beginning, with the development first of a psycho-analytically-based training for child care workers, and more recently of generic casework courses. I believe the day is coming when all case-workers will be expected to have a sound working understanding of the nature and manifestation of unconscious processes, the influence of early experience in relationship on the development of personality and on the relationships of later life, the nature and importance of ambivalence and its relation to the various forms of anxiety, and the mechanisms of defence by which we and our clients protect ourselves against our anxiety.

We must now consider how far the psychoanalytic technique, whose development went hand-in-hand with the theoretical discoveries, represents the only method by which such knowledge can be brought to bear on the solution of problems in personal relationships. It is probably inevitable that some of us who have experienced the benefits of personal analysis and have realized how similar are the problems which we take to our analysts and those which our clients bring to us, have been tempted to succumb to a feeling that analysis is the method par excellence of dealing with such problems, and to assume uncritically that the more our work could be made to resemble analysis the better it would be—despite the vigorous protests of numerous colleagues! It is time, however, that we cease to ignore these protests and to overlook the results achieved by other methods, and endeavour to see whether psychoanalytic theory cannot provide a frame of reference broad enough to accommodate traditional casework and various forms of psychotherapy as therapeutic methods alongside psychoanalysis itself. Freud himself envisaged that his own time-consuming technique (which has since his day developed into still more time-consuming forms) would require modification if the benefits of his discoveries were ever to be made available to any large proportion of those in need of psychotherapeutic help. Freud predicted in 1919[1] the development of a situation in which either the State or private institutions would accept responsibility for providing free 'analysis' for 'the men who would otherwise give way to drink, the women who have nearly succumbed under their burden of privations, the children for whom there is no choice but running wild or neurosis'. He does not in this context foresee that such therapeutic help might be given by non-medical workers, but he does explicitly envisage adaptation of technique. 'I have no doubt that the validity of our psychological assumptions will impress the uneducated too, but we shall need to find the simplest and most natural expression for our theoretical doctrines. . . . Possibly we may often only be able to achieve something if we combine aid for the mind with some material support. . . . It is very probable, too, that the application of our therapy to numbers will compel us to alloy the pure gold of analysis plentifully with the copper of direct suggestion. . . . But whatever form this psychotherapy for the people may take, whatever the elements out of which it is compounded, its most effective and most important ingredients will assuredly remain those borrowed from strict psychoanalysis which serves no ulterior purpose.'

I think the crucial difference between psychoanalytic technique (especially as developed by the English school of psychoanalysis) and that of other forms of psychotherapy, including casework, lies in the handling of *transference*. Some of us have been reluctant to make this differentiation; others have felt there was one, but have found it hard to formulate. Miss F. E. Waldron posed a number of very pertinent questions in 1948.

'A further development from our realization of our representative role may be our ability to stimulate our patient's growth beyond dependence without him transferring to us infantile emotional attitudes. We do not necessarily seek to avoid the "transference" situation, but if as social workers we consider we are not equipped to deal with the psychological mechanisms released by it, we must increase our aware-

[1] S. Freud, 'Turnings in the Ways of Psycho-Analytic Therapy,' *Collected Papers 2*, Hogarth Press, London, 1949, pp. 401-2.

ness of how we avoid it, and what help we substitute for the parental role. By examining a process which we have evolved intuitively we can make its application more valuable, for with knowledge about it we shall gain more control over it. If we do accept our role in a "transference" situation there is still need to examine it, for the course of a patient's growth from dependence on his social worker is probably different from that which developes from his "transference" to his doctor. The psychotherapists have examined their working relationship, have controlled it, and have taught social workers how to recognize and control the "transference" stage of their relationship with a patient. I think it possible that we are now in a position to show the psychotherapist that modifications and variations of the therapeutic relationship follow from the professional participator being a social worker, for we are bound to bring to the relationship qualities inherent in our approach that are distinctively ours and different from qualities found in therapeutic relationship between psychotherapist and patient.'[1]

I find that I agree with most of what Miss Waldron has said, provided we read 'psychoanalyst' for 'psychotherapist' (and with some reserve as to the extent to which either has taught the social worker how to control the development of transference). In the years since 1948, few of us have seriously tried to answer these questions, and most of those who made the attempt have given partial answers only, describing or illustrating each particular use of the relationship in which he was interested. Thus, some of us have been in favour of interpreting the transference (as far as our limitations of insight and training permit). Miss Lloyd Davies[2] agrees that the client tries to force transference roles upon us, but feels it is more appropriate to deal with this simply by resisting his attempts to manipulate us into playing these roles, and by asserting our own reality as distinct from these roles. This is a most important idea to which I shall return later. Mr Myers[3] and Miss Laquer[4] have published sensitive case material illustrating their own use of the relationship. Only Miss Goldberg,[5] I think, really tries to survey the *variety* of ways in which psychiatric social workers do in fact use their relationship with clients.

[1] F. E. Waldron, 'The Psychiatric Social Worker's Prefessional Standing,' *British Journal of Psychiatric Social Work*, Vol. I, No. 2, June 1948.
[2] op. cit.
[3] E. S. Myers, 'The Caseworker's Problems in Meeting the Inner and Outer Needs of Clients,' *British Journal of Psychiatric Social Work*, No. 10, October 1954, pp. 27-34.
[4] A. M. Laquer, 'The Caseworker's Task in Meeting the Client's Inner and Outer Needs,' *British Journal of Psychiatric Social Work*, No. 10, October 1954, pp. 22-6.
[5] E. M. Goldberg, 'Function and Use of Relationship in Psychiatric Social Work,' *British Journal of Psychiatric Social Work*, No. 8, 1953; and in this present book, pp. 95-107.

In this situation I have become uneasy about the signs that notions of 'orthodoxy' were developing; that colleagues spoke apologetically and defensively at meetings about methods of work which they clearly felt were appropriate to their clients and their settings, but unlikely to command respect from those who found more intensive methods appropriate in their own clinics. Experience in training caseworkers from a variety of fields, and continued contact with them after return to their own settings, have also led me to appreciate the value and necessity of variety. I now feel that we should stop thinking in terms of 'the right way to do casework' and recognize that analysed caseworkers can sometimes work in ways which are not appropriate for the unanalysed; that even so, these ways may not be appropriate for all clients and settings; and that we have reached a stage where it is less important to demonstrate what the analysed caseworker can do in favourable circumstances than to explore what the unanalysed can do with good training (because there are so many more of them, dealing with so many more clients).

What I want to attempt in this article is to construct a frame of reference within which we can formulate an account, consonant with Freudian theory, of the variety of ways in which we try to promote or facilitate emotional growth and development in clients, or to modify their attitudes and behaviour. How can one human being help another to change? I would like to begin by quoting Miss Pearl King[1] to the effect that the aim of many forms of casework and psychotherapy is to remove some of the obstacles to the inherent tendency of human beings towards healthy development. This formulation reminds us of the existence of spontaneous creative and recuperative tendencies in human beings, without which we, as caseworkers, could do little indeed. It parallels another fact which I would like to recall, which is that every relationship combines two elements in varying proportions:

(a) Response to the reality of the other person, with ability to perceive his qualities, and to feel and react appropriately. (Only with the psychotic is this element likely to be absent, and often then not completely so.)

(b) Transference, with its aspects of perceptual distortion, inappropriate emotion and manipulative action—its tendency to transform this present person and the present situation into the image and likeness of an earlier person and a past situation.

The more normal the subject, the more will (a) preponderate over (b) in spontaneous relationships. Nevertheless, some degree of transference is always present, and it can reach considerable intensity in a

[1] Personal communication.

H

casework situation, *whether client and worker recognize it or not.* In fact we are coming to realize that one reason why it is important for every caseworker to be able to recognize transference phenomena is that it is necessary to recognize them in order to be able to modify and control them.

Transference is of course a manifestation of unconscious phantasy, interfering with adaptation to reality. It occurs, as I have said more or less in all relationships, and notably in those disturbed relationships with family and friends with which the caseworker's help is so often sought. Any form of psychotherapy must therefore attempt to modify this distorting influence, so that the patient (or client) may become more discriminatingly adaptive. For this purpose psychoanalysts have come to rely increasingly on the interpretation of the transference to the therapist in both its positive and negative aspects, since it is through this transference that the therapist is in direct contact with the inner world of the patient's phantasy. It is probably true that this is the most effective way known to us of profoundly modifying this inner world; but it is not the only way of helping the individual to deal with unconscious phantasy, and of modifying its effect on current relationships. We all know that stable parents have their own way of helping children to deal with unconscious anxieties, by remaining benevolent and un-damaged, and by retaining a benign control of the situation; by being in fact actively parental. I think the best of the early caseworkers must have used their relationship with their clients in just this parental way. Octavia Hill, for instance, had the warmest maternal feelings for her clients, and never went to the country without bringing back in-numerable bunches of flowers for her enormous family. She offered to a very deprived and rejected group a relationship in which they could respond to her emotional warmth, learn to identify with her courage and self-confidence, and experience her genuine appreciation of their own capacity for response and self-help. Such attitudes seem to have worked remarkable changes in numbers of clients. They were not, however, easy to maintain; the early literature of social work contains much evidence of the struggle to walk this narrow way between the Scylla of over-indulgence (based on guilt towards the deprived and outcast) and the Charybdis of self-righteous contempt for the 'un-deserving' (based on paranoid anxieties about the danger of insatiable exploitation by these damaged clients).

I think there are still many situations in which it is appropriate for the caseworker (including the psychiatric social worker) to *play a parental role* in this traditional way, rather than to attempt to foster insight by interpreting the reflection of parental images as projected on to him by the client. In this type of casework the essential process lies in the acting out of a parent-child relationship between worker and client. A psychiatric social worker, describing her work with a number of immature psychopathic personalities in a mental hospital, recently gave a good description of just this sort of work, in which she sets the limits of what she could offer in terms of length and frequency of interviews like a firm and patient parent, showing sympathetic understanding of the wish for more attention, while holding to the limits she had set and explaining the need for these in terms of the needs of others with which she was also concerned. Miss Goldberg also quotes a very telling case of this kind in her paper on the use of relationship.[1] It concerned a young alcoholic with a weak character and weak, indulgent parents, who failed to take the drug which was an essential part of his treatment. The worker found it necessary himself to play the part of a strong, controlling father, and dramatized this at a crucial moment by insisting that the patient take a tablet there and then.

It is important to recognize that the playing of even a quite authoritative role such as this can be genuine casework, provided it is dictated by the needs of the client and the situation, and not by the worker's own need to assert himself; provided also that it is a genuine expression of the worker's concern for the client, and not of rejection. If we do not recognize such a carrying of authority as casework we are going to confuse and undermine such caseworkers as probation officers and child care workers, who must often of necessity play just such a role; it is better to admit that even the psychiatric social worker may have clients who not only need advice, but also the experience of contact with someone who is prepared to give unpalatable advice and take full responsibility for it. These will usually be the very weak and immature clients; we shall probably agree that it is a pity to give much advice to those who are capable of thinking out their own solutions and taking responsibility for their own decisions.

It seems to have been of a rather similar group of clients that Ratcliffe and Jones write in *Case Conferences*: 'Not only must the caseworker see the patient as a human being, but *he must also be allowed to see her as a human being*'[2] (my italics). She may mention some incident of her personal life; reveal her ignorance of some points, etc. This is an interesting observation, not the less so for being in striking contrast to the way in

---

[1] op. cit. (p. 104 in the present book).
[2] T. A. Ratcliffe and E. V. Jones, 'Intrinsic Casework in a Community Setting,' *Case Conference*, Vol. II, No. 10, March 1956.

which some of us in other settings have been trying to keep our own personalities in the background. It seems to be borne out by the experience of other workers in the community care service, and to apply also to the relationship established by Family Service Unit workers with their clients. The authors do not unfortunately give the reasons why they think this group of clients needs this kind of relationship; one can therefore only speculate, but my guess would be that they have such a florid and frightening phantasy life that they are apt to become scared of what they project on to the worker, unless he presents his own reality to them in pretty firm outline.

It is probably already clear that in the role-playing type of casework one cannot generalize about 'the caseworker's role', because the role must be adjusted to the needs of each client as assessed by the worker. I have illustrated variants of an authoritative role; an article by Miss Elkan[1] shows the worker playing a very different role, that of someone who is patient and accepting and concerned about the clients' own feelings, whatever they have done. The really fascinating thing in one case was the determined efforts of the clients to put this attitude to the test by producing sweets which were not for the children but for themselves, inducing her to sanction this by accepting a sweet, and then inviting her to inspect the ration books, knowing she would find that they had used the children's coupons. One feels that it was probably the fact that she could remain friendly and accepting after all this which enabled them to feel it worth while to keep in touch with the children.

This role-playing casework is not psychotherapy in Dr Sutherland's sense; but I think there is no doubt that for many simple immature clients it is more appropriate than psychotherapy, because they are not capable of gaining insight, and because for them what is acted out is so much more important than anything which can be said. This leads us on to consider other types of work, in which there may be much discussion of the mother-child relationship in relation to the mother's early experience, yet the real essence of the work may lie in something which is being tacitly acted out between worker and client. Miss M. H. Holmes recently published a study of work with a mother, in which at first glance the technique appears to have been to help the mother recall her own experience in each of the areas in which there were problems between herself and her children—fears, rebelliousness, separation, rejection, sex curiosity, clothes, sex rivalry—thus helping in many instances to convert projection into sympathetic identification. But

[1] I. Elkan, 'Interviews with Neglectful Parents,' *British Journal of Psychiatric Work*, Vol. III, No. 3, Spring 1956.

underneath all this, something was being acted out in the relationship: 'in response to the tolerant and accepting attitude of the psychiatric social worker and the clinic staff as a whole, the parent often becomes better able to tolerate herself, and hence other people.'[1] More specifically, the mother was allowed to express a great deal of aggression against the patient, and was at the same time told how much the child needed her help (the worker's confidence that she would help in spite of the hostile feelings being clearly implied). Until this point, the mother was hostile to worker and clinic, but she then became friendly and trustful. A little later the mother expressed her conflict about smacking the child (Lynda), and the worker interpreted that she was punishing in Lynda rebelliousness such as she herself had felt as a child, adding that ambivalence towards one's mother is natural and universal. I think this was a crucial moment in relation to the aim 'to work through her feelings of rejection, and to make her feel accepted herself.' It was this experience in the relationship with the worker which made it possible 'to build up her maternal, positive attitude to Lynda by allowing her to express her hostility against the child and by encouraging her to discuss her relationship to her own mother.'

There is a great deal in common between what went on in this case and in some cases described by Miss Betty Joseph in 1948—an article whose theoretical implications were not easy to assimilate at the time. Miss Joseph describes a young mother who was having trouble with an obstinate soiling child of 22 months. She was a controlling and meticulous person, who concealed a sensitive and meticulous personality beneath 'a tough defiant shell.' After a very few interviews in which the worker made contact with the mother's sensitivity and need for care, the child began to be less defiant about soiling, and to invite his mother to share his interest and pride in his motions. Miss Joseph writes: 'I have the impression that it was not only the child who was allowing himself to take a proud and friendly interest in his 'big jobs' with a 'nose'. . . . The mother's own deep interest in dirtying and anal habits, so much overlaid by her reaction-formation of over-cleanliness and tidiness, was being allowed some direct, or at any rate vicarious, expression.'[2] It is noteworthy that Miss Joseph, who is herself an analyst, gave very careful consideration to the question of whether the improvement obtained in some eight or nine interviews might be only a symptom improvement, and decided that there was real improve-

[1] M. H. Holmes, 'Mother and Child,' *British Journal of Psychiatric Social Work*, Vol. III, No. 3, Spring 1956.
[2] B. Joseph, 'A Psychiatric Social Worker in a Maternity and Child Welfare Centre,' *British Journal of Psychiatric Social Work*, Vol. I, No. 2, June 1948.

ment in the mother-child relationship, and in the mother's confidence as a mother.

In another case, Miss Joseph soon had the feeling that the mother 'was just like her own naughty, intolerant daughter of $2\frac{1}{2}$, who could brook no frustration or waiting, and who shouted and lost her temper'. Miss Joseph did not, however, try to show the mother these negative aspects of her personality, but helped her to rediscover and regain the feeling of pride and unity with her child which she had enjoyed during pregnancy. 'At the same time, this mother was able to continue to behave in her emotional and immature way without risk of provoking me or losing my interest, so that she gained in her relationship with me, on, so to speak, a rarefied and verbalized level, the control and support that she could not give to her child who behaved in somewhat the same way. Within two months the situation was transformed. The mother was proud and happy with Judy, and able to tolerate and laugh about naughtiness.'

In both these cases the mother was allowed to reveal and display to the worker interests and characteristics which she had been unable to tolerate in the child; the worker, 'on a rarefied and verbalized level,' acted out the part of an accepting and tolerant mother; the client then, partly by identification, became able to be similarly accepting and tolerant with herself and her child, the struggle between mother and child was dissolved, and the affection which had been blocked by this struggle was allowed to flow more freely. I am becoming increasingly convinced that this is the most important thing which happens in casework on a parent-child problem, whether we interpret or not; and I suspect that it applies, *mutatis mutandis*, to casework on any problem in relationship. For this reason the quality of the counter-transference is probably more important than the interpretation of the transference (although the *understanding* of the transference is very important for the control of the counter-transference). This brings me back to Ratcliffe and Jones. 'The caseworker must show herself as a human being who understands the particular difficulties that the client himself is experiencing as a human being. She cannot do this unless she has a genuine and sincere concern for him as a person. Assumed geniality will be seen through.'[1] It is interesting to compare Miss Joseph's comment that in the type of work described rapid changes can occur: 'if I can get a really deeply established contact with the mother, and if, in addition to intellectual understanding of the problem myself, I am able to get also an understanding of the feeling content of the situation.'[2]

[1] op. cit.   [2] op. cit.

I think this implies that in this sort of work the worker's own feeling response is an essential part of the help she gives the client. Insight, and the interpretations by which it is conveyed, may be very useful to certain clients; but just as we now believe that a particular method of feeding or training a child is less important than the attitude which the mother communicates by her *way* of using any method, so I believe that interpretations in general are less important than the caseworker's attitude, whether conveyed through interpretations or by other means. This is probably why different workers obtain satisfactory results with such a variety of techniques, and why any given technique can let us down if the counter-transference becomes predominantly negative.

If this is so, we can afford to relax our efforts to find 'the best' or 'the proper' amount or kind of interpretation, and focus more of our interest on the particular way in which each client wants to use the relationship and the interviews. Some have a very clear idea of the kind of problem they want to think out, whether it be something about a child which they want to understand or something in themselves. If they are allowed to set about this self-appointed task, they may do very good and useful work, using the worker as a supportive figure in much the same way as a young child learning to walk may use an adult's finger, not to take his weight, but to give him confidence and balance. In such a case, all that the worker needs to do is to give occasional evidence of continued interest and understanding, perhaps now and then verbalizing a little more clearly than the client something which was implied or hinted, or asking for clarification of some ambiguity. I think some of us have laid too much emphasis on interpretation and not enough on the value of the type of question which leads the client towards finding his own interpretation (as distinct from the 'fact-finding' question which is so often used to change a subject which one is reluctant to pursue). Questions directed towards clarification have the advantage of inducing (or allowing) the client to do more of the work, and this in turn limits the client's dependence on the worker, and reduces the conflict and resistance which arise from excessive dependence.

It is true that many clients want help on terms on which it cannot be given; they are apt, for instance, to limit somewhat arbitrarily the areas which they are prepared to discuss, and a time will come when we shall have to show them that the selected area cannot be understood without reference to excluded areas. If something worthwhile, but limited, can be done on the client's terms, it is often useful to do this first. For instance, a mother may say that she is prepared to discuss her relationship with the child who is the patient, but not the marital relationship, and provided she is prepared to include her own early relationships within the discussion, progress can be made; if a point is reached at which the marital relationship is clearly relevant, we must then find ways of helping the mother to see that this is so. I sometimes put it to a mother that she is entitled to refuse to discuss such problems with which she has not herself asked for my help, but that I want her to understand that this limits the help I can give her with the presenting problem. Sometimes the mother will then agree to widen the area of discussion; in other cases we may agree to terminate a treatment which has gone as far as she can allow. I have often found that a mother who is allowed to act out her resistance in this way may ask for more treatment after an interval; having found her own need, she will then take more responsibility for co-operating, and offer less resistance to the work.

Sometimes a mother's terms are less workable than this; she may, for instance, refuse to talk of her own early history, or even of her own feelings towards the child, on the grounds that the problem is all in the child, and that that is the only thing she is prepared to discuss—her own feelings have nothing to do with it. In many cases we cannot hope to give much help with the child's problem without some exploration of what is being displaced or projected on to it; but we may be able as a first step to give some relief to the anxiety behind the mother's wilfulness by sharing with her our understanding of the anxiety underlying the child's wilfulness. In general, if interviews are being used defensively, we shall have to find some way of making contact with the underlying anxieties, in which we ourselves and our anticipated reactions are bound to be involved.

If we are sensitized to transference, we shall certainly find a great deal of it in the client-worker relationship; its proportion in the total relationship varies considerably, and a strong transference is equally compatible with excellent co-operation and with great resistiveness. Where the transference is producing resistance, one has to do something about it, whether by interpretation or otherwise. In her paper, referred to above,[1] Miss Lloyd Davies gives some excellent examples of non-interpretive handling which I would consider first-rate casework. On the other hand, I do not myself share her anxieties about interpreting the transference, provided one can see it sufficiently clearly, and provided one can see both the positive and negative aspects, and is not misled into stressing one alone. I think it is useful as far as possible to

[1] op. cit.

keep one's style simple and natural: 'I believe you feel I am just as bad as mother,' or 'You pulled the wool over father's eyes, and I believe you are trying to pull it over my eyes too, aren't you?'

At this point I would like to distinguish between (a) the transference interpretation proper, of which these are very simple examples, which relates the immediate present situation to some infantile, or at least some earlier situation; and (b) the verbal recognition of feelings in the here and now situation which may be conscious or at least not far from consciousness, but which are denied, concealed or given only displaced and indirect expression (e.g. in terms of complaints against someone other than the therapist). This is something loosely called 'taking up the transference' or even 'transference interpretation', but I think the distinction is important.

The first (which we might call a 'now and then interpretation') has become the most highly valued form of analytic interpretation. Ana-lysed caseworkers can learn to use it skilfully, and I find that some unanalysed workers can learn to use the simpler forms, such as I have illustrated, on occasion; but I do not find it appropriate for all clients, and it cannot become a characteristic implement for a profession most of whose members are unanalysed. The second (which we might call a 'here and now interpretation') is something which I find useful with nearly all clients, and which I think all caseworkers could learn to use, given good selection and training for the profession.

I think we can now take up Miss Waldron's question[1] as to how we can control and limit the transference elements in the situation, if and when we want to do so. In general I believe that an interpretative tech-nique (like other elements of analytic technique) is an invitation to a partial suspension of ego function for the duration of the session, with a view to uncovering phantasy and stimulating transference. On the other hand, the use of devices, such as the question, which enlist the active co-operation of the client is stimulating to the ego and limits the activity of phantasy. For instance, when a client is talking defensively, it might be appropriate to say: 'You feel that I am accusing you of . . . ,' and to interpret this feeling as a projection. But it is also possible to say: 'You are talking as if someone had accused you of . . . and I wonder who it is? I don't think it is me.' This can often elicit some such response as: 'No, it's myself—that's what I feel.' In other words, the client himself can recognize the projection. Some forms of interpretation can convey a reassuring reference to reality: 'You find it hard to believe that I am not as critical as your mother.'

[1] op. cit.

Miss Joseph[1] deliberately saw the mother relatively infrequently; this is one way of limiting the importance one assumes for the client and the amount of phantasy one stimulates. It is clear that in the work described she welcomed and encouraged the client's independence, and let her do as much for herself as possible. (Again, one might say that she was acting out a certain kind of maternal relationship.) If a sudden dramatic improvement in the child made the mother feel as if the worker had done some magic, Miss Joseph dealt with this by appeal to the real situation, i.e. by helping the mother to see how much of the improvement was due to her own work.

This is a simple instance of a way of using the reality of the professional situation which is characteristic of the functional school of casework in America. It sometimes happens, for instance, that a client develops a strong ambivalent transference, and engages the worker week after week in discussing why he should continue to come. One may discern in this material very paranoid elements, together with a great deal of underlying positive feeling, and a demand for constant reassurance in the form of persuasion to continue attending. If one interprets all this, one is apt to get in very deep indeed; on the other hand, if we attempt to hold the client by stressing his need, or explaining the advantages of attending we are gratifying a neurotic need for repeated reassurance of being wanted, without doing anything therapeutic, and the situation tends to become static. The 'functional' way out of this impasse is to comment on the way the client is defining the situation, e.g. as one in which he is under moral pressure to attend for purposes of the worker's which are beyond his comprehension; and to contrast this with the actual situation in which the worker is trying to give him some help which he asked for. Has he in fact been pursuing this purpose or obstructing it? Is he still pursuing it? Has he already had the help he wanted, or has he lost hope of getting it? If the discussions have not been relevant to this purpose, has he or the worker been responsible? Does he really think this or that was so irrelevant? If he is really satisfied with the help he has had, why not stop coming? If, on the other hand, he is not satisfied, he is also free to stop coming; but it may be premature to despair of finding such help, and perhaps he has some suggestions as to the kind of discussion which might be more helpful.

To return from technical devices to essentials, I am now inclined to think that the basic element in casework consists in enabling the client to experience with the worker a kind of relationship which is new and

[1] op. cit.

helpful for him. I think it will always have to be one in which his ambivalence is recognized and accepted, and one which the worker is able both to understand and to resist the client's defensive attempts at manipulation. But in other respects it may vary considerably, so as to supply those experiences which may have been lacking in earlier relationships. If the transference is interpreted, I think the aim will usually be not so much to explore the inner world which is projected in the transference as to remove the veil of distortion and enable the client once more to experience the reality of the relationship; and I think Miss Lloyd Davies[1] has shown us that there are other methods of doing this. This new experience, in which old conflicts find to some extent a new resolution, may be combined to varying extents with insight-developing techniques such as the interpretation of transference within the family, which are extremely valuable for clients who have the necessary intellectual and emotional equipment to achieve such insight.

This way of looking at casework recognizes a basic continuity with its earlier forms, as practised by Octavia Hill and others. I think the contact with psychoanalysis should not induce us to relinquish this tradition of actively playing out the role of a parental figure such as the client needs to relate to, but should help us to manage the relationship more securely, more sensitively and skilfully so as to meet the needs of each client more precisely and more differentially. If we also aim to help the client develop insight, our casework will to that extent be classifiable as a form of psychotherapy; this psychotherapeutic casework may be more valuable for some clients, but not, I think, for all. For this purpose we may adopt various ingredients from analytic technique, and time will show which of these are most appropriate; but they must, I think, be subordinated to the characteristic casework way of using the worker-client relationship. In the long run I think we shall find that our debt to analysis in respect of deepened insight into ourselves and our clients far outweighs our debt in respect of technical borrowings.

[1] op. cit.

9

TYPOLOGIES FOR CASEWORKERS: SOME CONSIDERATIONS AND PROBLEMS*

LOLA G. SELBY

A NOBEL prize-winner for physics recently stated that the strength of Western culture stems from 'the close relationship between the way in which we pose our questions and our practical actions'. This author says that the ability of a people to change the questions asked into questions of principle—which in turn influence practical action—is what imposes order on 'the colourful kaleidoscope of experience' and leads to progress.[1]

How to phrase questions so that they become searching questions of principle is, of course, the crucial problem for researchers and scientists and a problem for members of any profession seeking to structure that profession's knowledge and experience. Social work has reached the stage in its development in which it sees professional education as involving teaching from generic concepts and principles rather than from a job-focused approach. Likewise social work research is moving from preoccupation with operational and administrative concerns to basic research, which undertakes to spell out social work culture and practice theory as well as to develop some helpful evaluative and measurement devices for the profession.[2] There are other indications, too, of social work's coming of age in the ways in which it poses its questions, conceptualizes and organizes its 'thoughtways', and defines its principles. For instance, the curriculum study carried out under the auspices of the Council on Social Work Education has sought not only to find out what is currently being taught in the schools but also to organize this content into a conceptual

* Published in *The Social Service Review*, Vol. XXXII, No. 4, December 1958.

[1] Werner Heisenberg, 'A Scientist's Case for the Classics,' *Harper's Magazine*, Vol. CCXVI, May 1958, pp. 25-9.

[2] Ernest Greenwood, 'Social Work Research: A Decade of Reappraisal,' *Social Service Review*, Vol. XXXI, September 1957, pp. 311-20.

framework for schools to use in their educational programmes in the future. Many persons would maintain that still another manifestation of professional progress is the movement towards developing some typologies to serve the purpose of supporting social work practitioners in their judgments and actions.[1] The purpose of this paper is to raise some of the questions that need to be asked and to identify some of the misconceptions and problems that can be anticipated in dealing with so complex a project as the development of typologies for social work—and for the casework field in particular.

Long a part of social science vocabulary, the term 'typology' has only recently begun to appear in social work literature, but there is increasing reference to it in current professional publications and at professional meetings.[2] The word 'typology', from the Latin 'typus' meaning 'impression; that by which something is symbolized', may soon become a part of every social worker's professional language. The development of typologies seems to follow logically the development of basic research, which in turn seeks to find answers to questions of principle and to organize ideas and knowledge.

As Greenwood points out, a well-developed practice has at its disposal highly refined diagnostic and treatment typologies that embrace the entire gamut of problems confronted by that discipline.[3] These classification schemes attempt to arrange according to natural relationships the phenomena with which the profession is concerned. To classify, according to the dictionary, is to identify 'a group of persons, things, qualities, etc., having common characteristics'. Factors that have some connection or items that are similar can be organized into a logical system that helps the user to identify or categorize facts, persons, or observations he is trying to understand. Typologies are a form of symbolic representation, aiding communication and common understanding by providing a profession with a kind of idealogical shorthand. Ready examples are the diagnostic and treatment typologies developed by the field of medicine which 'impart to medical practice

[1] Ernest Greenwood, 'Social Science and Social Work: A Theory of their Relationship,' *Social Service Review*, Vol. XXXIX, March 1955, p. 28.

[2] See the February-March 1958 issue of *Social Casework*, Vol. XXXIX, Nos. 2 and 3. Several articles therein either suggest particular classification schemes or stress need for their development. The subject of typologies is now frequently discussed in professional meetings of social workers. For instance, the April 1958 meeting of the Research Section of the Los Angeles NASW Chapter was devoted to a paper by Olive M. Stone on 'Diagnostic and Treatment Typologies for Social Workers' (mimeographed; available from Los Angeles Chapter of the National Association of Social Workers), with the author as discussant.

[3] Greenwood, 'Social Science and Social Work: A Theory of their Relationship,' op. cit., p. 28.

its relative specificity and to the medical practitioner his relative sureness'.[1] Greenwood and other members of the social work professions are beginning to recommend the construction of diagnostic and treatment typologies for social work. These classification schemes, as Greenwod indicates, would help practitioners to answer such a question as 'What *type* of action is indicated in a given *type* of situation to achieve a given *type* of goal?'[2]

This movement towards the development of classification systems for social work cannot be expected to proceed without some opposition from the field or without the necessity of clearing away popular misconceptions about typologies and their use. If an opinion poll were to be taken to explore the reactions of social workers to the idea of social work typologies, two quite opposite points of view (along with some mixed and middle-of-the-road responses) might be expected. One group, no doubt, would be strongly in favour of classification systems, indicating that, 'if we had such classifications, we could be much surer of ourselves and of what we are doing'. This attitude on the part of at least some members of the group favouring typologies would stem from the wish for a kind of magic formula or prescription to be applied in given situations with sure results. If only clients could be fitted neatly into a classification scheme, social workers would know with more certainty how to be helpful.

In all probability, another group of practitioners would shun typologies. These workers would see any attempt to 'type' clients or to designate treatment measures as opposing important social work principles—such as those principles related to individualization and self-determination. 'Typing' would be construed as an activity interfering with the dynamic interaction between worker and client, as well as a sure way of denying the client's impulse to maintain his own integrity, to change, or to pursue his own goals in his own way. The group of practitioners holding this point of view would undoubtedly associate typologies with stereotypes and, hence, would look dimly on applying labels or working towards prescribed solutions.

Another problem relating to construction and use of typologies would be the difficulty of setting up mutually exclusive categories. This difficulty is, of course, faced by any profession seeking to classify its knowledge and experience, because dichotomies and categories are seldom 'real' or complete in all respects. Social workers know that such dichotomies as environmental-internal situations, organic-functional problems, and direct-indirect treatment have their limitations in fact.

[1] ibid.   [2] ibid., p. 23.

No client's problem is exclusively external or internal, organic or functional. No treatment plan can deal exclusively with either conscious or unconscious factors. No diagnostic type will run true to form in every respect. To see only one aspect is to stratify or segment thinking, rather than to synthesize.

Medicine and psychiatry have extensive diagnostic typologies, but doctors experience difficulties in applying these categories because each 'case' has its own unique elements and because each situation may include some features common to other categories. It is difficult to be precise and at the same time indicate a general 'type'. In the field of psychiatry, for example, the American Psychiatric Association's classification system for childhood disorders includes a number of very broad categories and relatively few precise subcategories. Psychiatrists are still trying to formulate a better classification scheme for the behavioural and characterological difficulties known to childhood, but even if there were this scheme the typology in itself would offer no absolute assurance of exact diagnosis. In fact, it sometimes happens that different doctors assign different diagnostic categories to the same case, because categories are not mutually exclusive, and because different doctors draw different inferences from the symptoms displayed by the patient. It is worthy of note, however, that, despite these problems in the use of diagnostic typologies, the medical profession has generally found them to be useful and would not think of discarding them. There is, rather, continued effort to refine existent typologies in the light of new knowledge.[1]

It can be said, then, that the difficulties confronted by the social work profession, as it considers the development of typologies of its own, include the following: how to set up meaningful categories when categories cannot always be mutually exclusive; how to set up categories that will assist the user in synthesizing his thinking rather than stratifying or dichotomizing it; how to create typologies that will truly illuminate and not be used as 'magic formulas' or as 'gadgets'; how to construct typologies that will assist rather than inhibit the social worker in participating with the client in the creative and dynamic interaction that is the heart of social work process; how to learn to use typologies in ways that will still permit individualization of person and problem.

The answers to these questions will not be simple, nor will it be

[1] Some of the difficulties faced by psychiatry in defining and categorising patients' difficulties are discussed in *Current Problems in Psychiatric Diagnosis*, ed. Paul H. Hoch, M.D., and Joseph Zubin, Grune & Stratton, New York, 1953.

an easy task to decide what, within the broad province of social work, can really be categorized. In the field of casework, for example, where should one start in the search for common characteristics represented in a highly diversified clientele seeking solutions to an unlimited range of problems? Where does one begin to establish some 'classes' or categories?

There were several efforts a decade or more ago to classify casework procedures. For example, Hamilton, Austin, and Hollis of the New York group described 'levels of treatment' and categorized treatment techniques and methods. These writers utilized diagnostic categories from psychiatry as well as the social worker's special knowledge of environmental factors as a basis for discussion of treatment categories and methods. A similar approach was adopted by the Family Service Association of America in its 1953 statement on *Scope and Methods of the Family Service Agency* in which selection of treatment aims is discussed in relation to psychosocial diagnosis. More recent ideas about how to establish treatment goals have been included in the writings of the Smith College group on ego psychology and case-work theory. In this material, treatment objectives and methods are discussed in the light of personality diagnosis based on understanding of ego-functioning and the mechanisms of defence. No clear-cut treatment typology is suggested in this compilation of papers, but the treatment aims and techniques discussed stem from a particular theory of personality structure and behaviour.[1]

In a broader framework there have been some attempts to categorize or describe casework process in a structural way. Adherents of the functional tradition, while placing much emphasis on dynamic inter-action between worker and client and while minimizing the use of diagnostic typologies, do nevertheless structure the casework process in terms of beginning, middle and end phases and in terms of what characteristic client reactions can be anticipated at different stages in the process. There is also the Pittsburgh outline which employs the familiar Richmond formula of 'study-diagnosis-treatment' and de-scribes each step, spelling out the principles involved.[2] Another

[1] See Gordon Hamilton, *Theory and Practice in Social Case Work*, Columbia University Press, New York, 1951; Lucille N. Austin, 'Trends in Differential Treatment in Social Casework,' and Florence Hollis, 'The Techniques of Casework,' in *Principles and Techniques in Social Casework*, ed. Cora Kasius, Family Service Association of America, New York, 1950. See also *Scope and Methods of the Family Service Agency*, Family Service Association of America, New York, 1953; and *Ego Psychology and Dynamic Casework*, ed. Howard J. Parad, Family Service Association of America, New York, 1958.

[2] *A Conceptual Framework for Social Casework*, 2nd ed., University of Pittsburgh Press, 1956.

example of the structuring of casework process appears in Helen Perlman's important volume on social casework as a problem-solving process. Therein the social casework situation is looked at within the structure of person-problem-place-process, and the author's ideas regarding content and method are applied to the 'beginning phase' of problem-solving.[1]

Efforts to establish diagnostic categories that reflect casework or social work orientation have been slow in evolving. Thus far caseworkers have for the most part been content to borrow the diagnostic typologies already developed in the fields of medicine and psychiatry, with perhaps a few categories from the social sciences thrown in. Even so there has been no common agreement on the theory of personality development and behaviour to be utilized in personality assessment, and there has been no common agreement on other elements that should enter into diagnosis or influence the taxonomies. One might ask, then: Is it possible to develop a diagnostic typology that reflects a social work approach exclusively, or will it always be necessary to employ typologies and systems of knowledge from other fields? Can there ever be agreement on what should be included in diagnostic typologies for social work? And if social work typologies *are* set up to assist in casework diagnosis, how will they affect the social worker's 'practical actions'?

It seems probable that, since social work has to do with human behaviour, whatever is learned in any field about behaviour and the nature of man will eventually have an effect on the development of social work. At the same time it does seem important for social workers to incorporate this material into their own distinctive thought-ways and to devise their own thought-systems. As Greenwood points out, a typology of behaviour disorders borrowed 'as is' from psychiatry does not meet the need, because caseworkers are not psychiatrists and their principal business is not psychopathology. Greenwood adds that 'if casework has a unique function, as caseworkers so insistently contend, it must have its own diagnostic and treatment typologies'.[2]

There are some moves towards the development of diagnostic typologies for caseworkers. Ripple and her associates have devised a problem-classification scheme which they think may serve as an aid to better understanding of the 'person-in-the-situation'—as caseworker and client come together to explore what is needed and what possibly

[1] Helen Harris Perlman, *Social Casework: A Problem-solving Process*, University of Chicago Press, Chicago, 1957.
[2] Greenwood, 'Social Science and Social Work: A Theory of their Relationship,' op. cit., p. 28.

I

can be done in relation to the problem. The Chicago Research Centre studies have opened up the whole area of 'motivation, capacity, and opportunity' and their relationship to problem-solving. Findings from this research, when completed and more widely circulated, should provide some important ideas for the development of other and more extensive typologies for casework.[1]

Werner Boehm, in speaking at the 1958 Council on Social Work Education meeting in Detroit, presented the role concept as one kind of useful classification system. He listed a number of activities and tasks the individual is required to perform in our society, and suggested that study of the roles the individual is assuming (or avoiding) in his life-situation can provide diagnostic clues about the extent and quality of the individual's social interaction. This particular categorization, a social work adaptation of a social science typology, reflects an important current trend towards incorporating more social science concepts into social work thinking and practice.[2]

There is also considerable interest in 'family diagnosis' which, in the words of Gomberg, recognizes the 'interdependence between individual diagnosis and family diagnosis, between socio-cultural factors and psychological factors, and between the treatment of the individual's failures in adjustment and adaptation and treatment of the family.[3] A number of students of 'the family' are trying to construct typologies classifying such particulars as 'family types' and 'stressor events' which affect family interaction. A related pursuit is represented in Ackerman's conceptual scheme for evaluating neurotic marital interaction.[4]

Some efforts at diagnostic categorization have also occurred in the context of social work education. There has been considerable thinking

[1] Lilian Ripple and Ernestina Alexander, 'Motivation, Capacity, and Opportunity as Related to the Use of Casework Service: Nature of Client's Problem,' *Social Service Review*, Vol. XXX, March 1956, pp. 38-54. Ripple points out that the various classification schemes contrived in the past have 'evolved into check lists whose categories are not mutually exclusive but, further, may describe problems, solutions, requests, services, causes, consequences, conditions, or mere statements of status'. Ripple gives credit to Towle for ideas leading to the development of the problem-classification scheme in the MCO study. Towle had long considered motivation, capacity, and opportunity as significant variables in contrasting 'learners' and 'non-learners' in the educational setting. See footnote to Ripple's article on 'Plan of Study,' *Social Service Review*, Vol. XXXIX, June 1955, p. 174.

[2] Werner W. Boehm, 'The Curriculum Study: Highlights and Prospects,' *Education for Social Work: Proceedings of Sixth Annual Program Meeting, Council on Social Work Education, Detroit, Michigan, January 29-February 1, 1958*, pp. 32-50.

[3] M. Robert Gomberg, 'Family Diagnosis: Trends in Theory and Practice,' *Social Casework*, Vol. XXXIX, February-March 1958, p. 73. Reprinted in *Social Work with Families*, compiled by Eileen Younghusband, Allen & Unwin, London, 1965, p. 150.

[4] Nathan W. Ackerman, M.D., 'The Diagnosis of Neurotic Marital Interaction,' ibid., Vol. XXXV, April, 1954, 139-47.

about selection of students for schools of social work and the relationship between educational process and social work process. Charlotte Towle's monumental work, *The Learner in Education for the Professions*, sums up her thinking, developed over many years, about educational diagnosis and criteria of educability. She suggests a typology for use by schools in selecting students for admission. A related effort, having to do with students' learning patterns, appears in a report on a study at the New York School of Social Work.[1]

These diagnostic typologies constructed primarily for use by social workers all seem to derive from the social work point of view that the individual is a social being whose behaviour reflects his relationships and strivings as well as the influence of both internal and external factors in his life-situation. An effort is made to take into account the person-situation constellation and to get at how the person in the situation operates 'with, through, and in spite of internal and external forces'.[2] To try to categorize or classify so many complicated and interrelated factors when there are so many variables is a large order, but to include less coverage in diagnosis is perhaps to lose perspective or limit understanding to one-dimensional considerations.

Caseworkers are interested in helping clients find relief from environmental and/or emotional pressures. Such questions as how to help clients make use of their own adaptive capacities in resolution of their problems and utilize their own strengths and resources for problem-solving are matters of professional concern to the caseworker. These casework tasks or goals seem to imply that diagnostic typologies for caseworkers must take into account what Olive Stone refers to as the client's 'directional aims and efforts'; there must also be consideration of the client's characteristic adaptive mechanisms, his own ways of striving toward his goals. What about the client's usual pattern of coping with stress or meeting life's daily demands? What about his current functioning, his usual problem-solving behaviour? What does he identify as 'the trouble'? What meaning does the situation have for him? Who or what contributes to the problem or can serve as a resource in the solution? What kind of help does the client want from the worker or agency? What motivates him to seek help, how much does he want to alter his situation, and what capacity

---

[1] See Charlotte Towle, *The Learner in Education for the Professions*, University of Chicago Press, 1954, chap. vi. See also Sidney Berengarten, 'Identifying Learning Patterns of Individual Students: An Exploratory Study,' *Social Service Review*, Vol. XXXI, December 1957, 407-17.

[2] Olive M. Stone, op. cit. Her suggested diagnostic typology, which employs both social science and social work concepts, is designed to help the worker determine (in the words of Harry Stack Sullivan) what the human entity with the problem is trying to do.

has he for utilizing help? What can worker, agency, and community offer to this person-in-the-situation? These are the kinds of questions the caseworker must seek to answer in order to understand his client and to carry out his professional responsibilities.

Is it possible to devise a single diagnostic classification system that will cover all of these considerations? This does not seem feasible. There would be so many facets of personality, behaviour, and problem to identify, so many categories and sub categories necessary, that the caseworker might never be able to untangle his own 'system', and the client's personality and activity might be lost behind a haze of 'factors'. There remains the possibility of constructing several relatively simple classifications, each emphasizing a particular facet or area of diagnostic concern, each throwing light on some important element of diagnostic inquiry. Singly or in combination these several usable typologies could enlarge the scope of the worker's thinking and understanding, deepen his perceptions, and illuminate his professional endeavours. One writer suggests that 'an adequate diagnostic classification will have to provide three independently useful components: (1) a personality classification; (2) a family-environmental classification; (3) a crisis-problem classification'.[1] Undoubtedly there are other components that may become apparent and seem important as consideration is given to the caseworker's necessary concerns and tasks, and as social work research is further developed. The construction of typologies should derive from and contribute to both practice and research. Diagnostic typologies should reflect what the caseworker needs to understand in order to be helpful; treatment typologies should be related to the caseworker's unique function, should reflect the profession's answer to the basic question, 'What is social casework?'

To sum up, there seems definitely to be a need in social work for further structuring of professional knowledge in order to convey it more effectively to others in the process of professional education and collaboration and in order to help practitioners apply professional concepts, generalizations, and classifiable information in appropriate ways. The systemization of knowledge can lend clarity and precision to professional thinking and activity. The phrasing of 'questions of principle' can lead to productive practical actions. It is time for social workers to augment the case method of learning and teaching with the use of tested generalizations and with the application of some

---

[1] Dorothy Fahs Beck, 'Research Relevant to Casework Treatment of Children: Current Research and Study Problems,' *Social Casework*, Vol. XXXIX, February-March 1958, p. 107.

carefully constructed typologies. No doubt the development of typologies will come slowly, however, because they are very difficult to construct and because the profession of social work has what Eileen Blackey calls a 'case-focused tradition'. She comments that this tradition 'has kept us in educational blinders and has often limited us to the specifics of the individual case in supervision, staff training, and professional education'. She quotes Charlotte Towle as saying that social casework teaching has long emphasized the uniqueness of each case situation and that this has entrenched an attitude of not daring to generalize.[1]

Many casework practitioners sincerely believe that diagnostic typologies in particular (or any kind of diagnostic labels) can do an injustice to the client by providing a worker-oriented rather than a client-focused approach to helping. These workers see classifying as to type, as a first step toward taking over responsibility for the outcome of treatment—a responsibility which really belongs to the client rather than to the worker. These practitioners would have to rid themselves of the fear of stereotyping and controlling before they could conceive of typologies as useful. Just as some practitioners would have to get over an aversion to 'ready-made labels', so other practitioners would have to learn to refrain from too-eager use of diagnostic typologies for labelling and too zealous use of treatment typologies for preplanned approaches mechanically administered without regard for individual difference and client self-determination.

Somewhere, somehow, social workers should be able to find the golden mean and should be able to establish some groupings of 'cases' and case problems into diagnostic typologies that truly reflect common features and at the same time leave room for the variables and for the individual features of the 'person-in-the-situation'. This should not destroy the art in casework, nor ignore the spirit, the goals, the integrity of the individuals being served. Typologies, if constructed with reference to the professional task at hand, should be illuminative and hence should contribute to effective helping efforts.

Helen Perlman states the purpose of the diagnostic process and

[1] Eileen A. Blackey, *Group Leadership in Staff Training*, Bureau of Public Assistance Report No. 29, Government Printing Office, Washington, D.C., 1957, pp. 35-8. It should be noted that Charlotte Towle long ago recognised the problems of generalisation in teaching and practice. In her article, 'Teaching Psychiatry in Social Case Work,' *Family*, Vol. XX, February 1940, pp. 324-30, she deals with this matter. Refer also to her introduction and teaching notes in *Social Case Records from Psychiatric Clinics*, University of Chicago Press, 1941. From each case discussed therein, she attempted to extract principles and concepts that might be transferred for use elsewhere. The subject of generalising from specifics is again dealt with in *The Learner in Education for the Professions*.

product in casework as being 'to give boundary, relevance, and direction to the caseworker's helpful intent and skills'.[1] Treatment which 'feels' helpful to the client, which enables him to resolve some of his difficulties or make some choices of action, is predicated on the worker's adequate understanding of the person and the problem. The caseworker, in order to be helpful, must assess the situation, draw some inferences from the facts, grasp the significance of the feelings involved, get some idea of what help is wanted—in other words, go through a mental process known as diagnosis. What the social worker does with this understanding reflects his concept of his role and professional responsibilities and his recognition of what kind of help might be appropriate in the given situation. The idea of differential treatment stems from the belief that helping efforts must be adapted to the needs and desires of the 'person-in-the-situation' and to 'the question for solution', to borrow phrases from Ripple. If social caseworkers can come to some agreement about what they need to know (i.e. diagnose) in order to ensure boundary, relevance, and direction for their helping efforts, then the profession will have some clues for diagnostic typologies that will be useful in practice. These should lead to the development of related treatment typologies based on understanding of the caseworker's function as a helping person. With social work typologies once constructed, it seems reasonable to believe that social workers will learn to apply them flexibly and creatively in their work with people.

[1] Perlman, op. cit., p. 179.

10

CASEWORK TECHNIQUES IN THE CHILD CARE SERVICES*

CLARE WINNICOTT

WHILE it is true to say that there are basic techniques by means of which we practise casework in any field in which it is applied, it is, nevertheless important to realize that techniques are always being altered and improved upon. They are not fixed and final but must remain flexible and capable of adaptation not only to the needs of individuals but to the setting in which they are being performed. The most important thing about techniques is their flexibility, for if they lose it and are allowed to harden they will soon cease to be effective instruments and become weapons for defence or attack in the hands of those who use them. This is always a potential danger in our work.

One of the difficulties about improving casework skill is that the knowledge derived from one experience cannot just be applied as it stands to the next case. This specific knowledge will never be required in just the same form again. It will only be of value in so far as it adds up to something in us, enriches our general understanding of human beings (including ourselves), and increases our confidence in our techniques. In this way a particular experience becomes part of ourselves and part of the professional equipment we take with us as we move on to the next case. The point is that we shall be better people in the new situation—we shall not have just learned a new trick.

Perhaps it is true to say that basic techniques, although they are derived from the specific, can be seen to exist only in theory and in relation to the general for in practice, in the live casework situation, they become part of the professional relationship absorbed in the

* Published in *Case Conference*, Vol. I, No. 9, January 1955.

experience and implicit in all that is done, rather than applied to what is done.

This does not mean that I am suggesting that casework is not a highly self-conscious business. It must always be more and more so. I am suggesting, however, that only as the worker becomes unaware of her techniques as such in her contact with the client will she be free to be self-aware and self-conscious and will her work be truly dynamic and productive. I know that this is all very obvious, but I find that I have to keep reminding myself of it as I talk about techniques, otherwise I can easily find myself believing in them as if they were a kind of formula which gives the required answer and solves the problem. And I have to remind myself that this is not so. Techniques are only ways of doing things within the framework of a professional relationship and in a given setting.

The presenting problem of work in the child care setting can be fairly clearly and broadly defined in terms of 'environmental breakdown involving the child'. It is this environmental factor which differentiates the service from that of other casework agencies and sets a pattern for the role of the caseworker.

Of course casework in the child care service merges at many points with that of other agencies, particularly with family casework agencies, child guidance clinics, and the probation services; and as workers in the child care field concern themselves more and more with the prevention of family breakdown, their work becomes more similar to that done by family caseworkers. I shall not discuss this preventive aspect of the service here although I am very much aware of its significance for the future development of casework in the child care setting. I shall concern myself with the work done for children who are in fact deprived of a normal home life, because this work is the especial concern and responsibility of the child care worker.

I should like to discuss briefly:

(1) The impingement of the environmental factor on the casework process;

(2) The nature of the professional relationship which is the child care worker's basic technique for doing her job;

(3) Casework with children, foster parents and parents, for it is in these three sets of relationships that the fullest use of casework skill is demanded.

I remember clearly how, when I moved from working in a child guidance clinic setting to working in a children's department of a local authority, the whole emphasis of my work changed. No longer was it concerned with working towards adjustments within a given environment (of course the environment could always fail or break down—but at least it was there to work with). In the child care setting the environmental breakdown was a fact and became the focal point of the work, and the immediate question often was 'where is this child to sleep tonight?' And to provide a roof and someone who could care for and manage the child was the first responsibility. No matter how carefully the work is planned so that breakdowns can be anticipated and plans worked out and worked through, the fact remains that the child care worker will always be exposed to the sudden crisis or emergency and will have to take immediate responsibility for the environment. She will find herself in action, rather than in her more familiar role of enabling people to act and think for themselves, and in her subsequent casework with the child she will have to spend time working backwards, explaining her action and helping the child to come to terms with it and with her. This is very different from the usual method of working forward—so that action is understood and accepted and the momentum to put it through is gathered together for the event.

This 'working backwards' is a modification of casework technique which is often imposed by the environmental factor in child care work. (By that I mean the direct responsibility to provide environment which devolves on the child care worker.) Of course other caseworkers are called upon to help clients to work backwards over previous experiences in order to come to terms with the present, but unlike the child care worker they have not been the centre of the drama as the actual people who have acted. Thus, it is easier in other situations for the client to talk about difficult experiences because the caseworker has not been involved in them.

Not only does the child care worker need to work backwards over situations in which she has had to take precipitate action but she has to deal with the fact that she is a person who holds the power to change an environment. This always complicates her casework relationships and must be talked about and worked through with children, parents and foster parents, and the staff of children's homes. For the child care worker is not just the accepting understanding person that they need her to be and which she wants to be, she is also a powerful person who can be a threat or a saviour, according to individual attitudes, needs, and circumstances. Unless she fully recognizes the implications of this fact and carefully explains her function, and at times brings into the open the possibility that she may be felt as a threat or a saviour, she will find her relationship confused and difficult to handle. I remember a girl of thirteen whom I had placed success-fully in a home two years previously, who suddenly began to avoid me and would slip out at the back door as I came in the gate. The foster mother told me that she was terrified that I would take her away. Although I had always had a good relationship with this child, it was obvious that the happier she became in the home and the more she valued it, the more of a threat did I appear to be. This had to be talked over with her repeatedly until she could gradually tolerate my visits again.

It is important that the child care worker should come to terms with her own power and responsibility in relation to the environment. Of course she can always avoid the issue by placing the power to act firmly on to a committee or senior official, but this does not solve her casework problem, for even if decisions are made at a higher level she must take responsibility for them in relation to her own cases, for it is she who must carry out the plan. If she is not to avoid the issue but is willing to take responsibility for her actions, the worker must be able to know about her own guilt feelings in relation to the power and responsibility she carries. She must be able to tolerate her guilt at depriving parents of their children as well as children of their parents, and she must be able to avoid dealing with her guilt by feeling that she is rescuing or saving children from a bad environment in order to provide them with a better one of her own choosing. The rescue motive is to be avoided in social work.

The environmental factor complicates the casework relationship and requires the modification of casework techniques in yet another way. The child's primary need is not for a casework relationship but for an environment which can provide for him and within which he can be cared for successfully. The main therapeutic experience for the child will not be in the relationship with the caseworker but in his relationships with his foster parents. Of course, the caseworker will be needed to help the child to deal with his feelings about his own parents and to adjust to and make use of his foster home; as well as to select and support the foster parents. Casework of a higher order will be required to do this part of the work.

With older children who are unable or do not need to make use of a foster home as a home (as young children do) the situation is dif-ferent. With them, the relationship with the caseworker will very often be of greater value and importance than the placement relation-ships. They will establish the caseworker-client relationship with which we are familiar, except that the worker's power and responsibility to act in relation to the environment will also be present and must be made explicit if necessary.

I should like to add one word about the source from which the child care worker derives her power to act in relation to the environment. It is surely derived from the constructive integrating forces in society. The desire is that all children shall have as good a home life as possible. The direct motive, therefore, is not punitive or educational or to make the children healthier; it is the simple straightforward motive of attempting to meet their need for love and happiness. The power, therefore, expresses the love and sense of parental responsibility that exists in society towards children.

Our professional relationship is in itself the basic technique, the one by means of which we relate ourselves to the individual and to the problem. But what of the professional self that relates? If we look at it objectively we find that it is the most highly organized and integrated part of ourselves. It is the best of ourselves, and includes all our positive and constructive impulses and all our capacity for personal relationships and experiences organized together for a purpose—the professional function which we have chosen. In other words, it is a function of the super ego, with which the ego has easily identified because it has evolved from loving identifications with early parental figures. Of course if there is a pathological super ego development based on fear of demanding parents rather than on identification with loving parents, we shall make impossible demands on ourselves and on others and shall fail as caseworkers.

In our professional relationship then we give the best part of ourselves, and when we ask the question what do we get out of them we find that it is a very great deal and fundamental to our well-being, and our continuing ability to do our work.

Briefly, we get a fundamental reassurance about our value and goodness—because people can take and use what we give. We get the chance to contribute to the world through our professional function and thereby relate ourselves to society and feel more secure in it. By giving we get the ability to tolerate our guilt feelings (because we all feel that we owe a debt for life itself and for our own greed and what we have demanded and taken from others). Thus our work helps us to achieve a balance between the constructive and destructive, positive and negative, good and bad sides of our nature (as with all chosen constructive work). Our professional relationships are more balanced and more reliable than our personal ones, and it is important that they should be. We look to our personal relationships for the satisfaction of our personal need for relationships—for instinct satisfaction. (By instinct satisfaction I mean the need to love and be loved in a personal intimate way). Personal relationships are, therefore, less reliable because they are subject to our needs and demands, to our moods and our jealousies and rivalries.

If our personal needs do intrude into our professional relationships difficulties of all kinds can arise. For one thing we shall be frustrated in both sets of relationships and in the long run we shall fail in practice because we are out of touch with the needs of other people. Moreover, we are liable to exploit the needs of others for our own personal satisfaction; for example we may continue to supervise an older boy or girl long after there is a need to do so and when we should be helping them to gain independence from us; we may stop supervision when there is a need for it because we cannot tolerate failure or lack of response. It feels too much like a personal rejection and we become hurt and frightened and hostile ourselves. The need to be loved and liked personally always makes us afraid of hostility and so we may placate people instead of taking and working through their hostility. If we are looking for personal love ourselves we can be jealous of a child's love of a foster mother, or intolerant of a mother who rejects the love of her child.

In so far as we offer our clients a personal relationship and not a professional one we fail them, because it is our professional relationship which is of more use to them and which they need in order to establish their own relationships on a more satisfactory basis.

I have said that the professional relationship is in itself the caseworkers' basic technique and I have said something about the nature of the relationship and how it affects the work. I should now like to try and put into words what I think the technique actually is. I think it lies in the provision of a reliable medium within which people can find themselves or that bit of themselves which they are uncertain about. We become, so to speak, a reliable environment which is what they so much need; reliable in time and place—and we take great trouble to be where we said we would be at the right time. The time factor is important in another way too, in that it limits the duration of the relationship. From the beginning we are working for the end and that helps us to tolerate the demands made on us. The client also knows that he is not making a relationship for life and that we shall not enter his personal world—and he is, therefore, more free to make demands on us and express his feelings because we give him a limited, but reliable, amount of time for a period only.

We are not only reliable in time and place but in the consistent attitudes which we maintain towards people. They know how they will find us. Here again we take deliberate trouble to remember all the details about a client's life and not to confuse him with other cases. We can 'hold' the idea of him in our relationship so that when he sees us he can find that bit of himself which he has given us. This is conveyed by the way in which we remember details and know exactly where we left him in the last interview. And not only do we hold a consistent idea of people, but we hold the difficult situation which brought the client to us by tolerating it until he either finds a way through it or tolerates it himself. If we can hold the painful experience recognizing its importance and not turning aside from it as the client relives it with us in talking about it, we help him to have the courage to feel its full impact; only as he can do that will his own natural healing processes be liberated.

I have deliberately used the word 'hold' in what I have been saying, because while it obviously includes 'acceptance' of the client and what he gives us it also includes what we do with what we accept.

To sum up, the professional relationship is the technique whereby we provide a limited and enclosed environmental setting which is personal because it contains all that the client has put into it himself, and which is reliable because it is accepting and holding. Through it the natural integrating processes are given a chance. This integrating function of the relationship is particularly important in working with children who have been moved from one home to another and have never known a continuing environmental setting.

Recently a child care worker was discussing the possibility of a new placement with a 16-year-old girl who had been in her care for a long time. The child expressed a wish to go and live near the matron of a hostel where she had once lived, adding: 'You know I think that Auntie Mary (the Matron) is the only person I've ever really loved.' After a pause she went on to say: 'Oh, except you of course, but you're different if you know what I mean.' The child was really showing that she recognized the difference between a personal and a professional relationship and that she could make use of both.

I said earlier that the main therapeutic experience for children deprived of a normal home life will be in the foster home or children's home in which they are placed. In other words it is in the environment that their need for personal relationships must be met. But the caseworker will be needed by the child to help him to make use of his foster home by talking over his new experiences and relating them to his own home and what has gone before, thus preserving a thread of continuity for him.

In her first contact with the child, whether it is in his own home or in a Reception Home, the worker must explain who she is and why she came and what she hopes to do for him. In doing this she must talk in detail about the event which led to her coming, why the child's own parents cannot keep him any longer, where they are, and when he can expect to see them again. These simple explanations must be given straight away even to very young children and even if they appear not to be listening or understanding. In subsequent interviews these explanations may have to be repeated over and over again together with any new facts about himself and his feelings which the child may contribute to the conversation. The main area of our casework with children will always be around their parental relationships, and our acceptance of their love of parents who have perhaps seriously failed them is all important if we are to save their capacity to love for future relationships. We must also know about their anger towards, and their disappointment in their parents, and how those feelings increase the pain of separation. These feelings must also be talked about with the children when they give us the opportunity, as they will if they trust us, and if we have established the sort of relationship in which they know they can be themselves and say what they feel without shocking us or risking losing us.

Child care workers sometimes feel that they have done their job in regard to parental relationships by arranging for the parents to maintain contact by visiting. As we know, these visits can cause much confusion and difficulty for the child, for what really matters is not the visits themselves, but what the parents are like when they visit. And I do not simply mean how did they behave but what sort of people are they fundamentally. Because this is the child's real problem, and one with which he will need all the help that we can give him. There may very well be times when the child should be protected from his parents' actual visits, but he will always need to know that the worker is available, and that he can talk to her about them at any time, and thus gradually come to terms with his feelings.

A case recently came to my notice of a 13-year-old boy whose mother had died when he was 3 and who had lived ever since in a foster home where the father was also a lodger. One day when he was $12\frac{1}{2}$ the father went away with no explanation to the boy and then after some weeks reappeared with a wife, having settled down to live in another town. In the meantime the boy had been received into the care of the local authority but remained in the same foster home. The father then wanted the boy to go and live with him in the new house, and everyone concerned felt this to be the best plan—except the boy, who said to the child care worker, 'If you make me go and see my father I'll be ill.' When the day came for him to go and visit his father who hoped to be able to persuade him to stay the boy was in fact ill. What was urgently needed in this case was for everyone to stop trying to manage the external situation and for the worker to apply the casework technique of helping the boy to put into words his feelings about his father. By recognizing the boy's underlying anger with his father (which found expression in terms of illness) and by giving him the opportunity of expressing it more fully the worker could give him the chance of eventually getting to his positive feelings, for he was in fact deeply attached to the father. The jealousy of the new wife would have to be talked about too, and the love of his foster mother and the conflict of loyalties which that aroused.

Of course these interpretations or verbalizations or whatever we call them do not immediately solve problems but they are the first step towards the possibility of a solution. They give to the child the feeling that somebody sees his point of view and understands and can tolerate his feelings, whatever they are.

In order to illustrate further the use of casework techniques in relation to children in care I should like to quote parts of two case records.

The first concerns Jean, a girl of 16 who was committed to the care of the local authority by the juvenile court. This interview is the first contact of a new child care worker with Jean who had been in care for a few weeks and had proved very difficult. The worker was suddenly called in to deal with a crisis over a new job.

This first interview lasted over an hour. Jean appeared in the sitting room untidy, sullen and apparently determined not to enter into any conversation. I introduced myself and began to talk about the court hearing, telling her of the work of the court officials, explaining the meaning of a fit person order and telling her how the county council entered into the picture. I talked about the children's department—our work—our place as her legal guardians, what we might be able to do to help her, how she could help build up her own life free from home ties, how some people were always happiest living away from their own families especially as they grew older and wanted to be independent, how I expected she wondered why the hostel had asked me to call—all this said in a friendly casual conversational manner, not expecting her to say anything in reply.

Gradually she showed signs of taking some interest and eventually I said I expected she had wondered what I would be like. Jean smiled and said: 'Yes, I thought you'd come to tell me off because I won't work on the farm.'

I replied that there didn't seem to be much point in her taking a job she didn't like, and that if she didn't want to stay at the pie shop we would have to look around and see what other kinds of work were available. Jean's reaction was immediate—she said she wanted to work on the farm, but her granny said she oughtn't to change her job again so soon and that she didn't approve of her working on Sundays. I asked if it would help if I saw her grandmother to explain matters. Jean brightened and said it would, and then her face clouded—she became sullen and said she didn't want to change her job.

I then said that working on a farm was very different from kitchen work and I wondered if she felt it was too big a change to make and perhaps she was looking ahead wondering what would happen if she didn't like the farm. Jean looked up quickly and said: 'They'd make me stay there, wouldn't they?'

I said no, I thought that the farmer would probably like her to go for a week or two's trial and then if she didn't like it she'd be able to leave.

Jean thought about this and then remarked anxiously: 'But he might not like me, then would I have to go?' I answered her in a non-committal tone: 'Well, he'd hardly keep you, if you played him up, would he?' Jean caught my eye and grinned. She said: 'You'd have to tell me off then, wouldn't you?' I said: 'Certainly,' and we both laughed. Jean's manner changed, she became bright and friendly, eager to discuss the new job.

Obviously the attitude of the worker had been all-important in establishing this contact. The worker's manner was friendly and conversational, with no hint of criticism, her approach to the job problem was objective, with no pressure brought to bear on Jean one way or the other; the relationship was not forced and the explanations were given with no effort to evoke a response. Then as Jean relaxed the worker took the opportunity of making a direct link between herself and the child by putting into words what had obviously been in Jean's mind about the worker, that is to say, what she was like and what she had come for. As the conversation continued on a realistic basis about the job, Jean was able to come to grips with it and, with the worker's help, to express her fears and explore the possibilities and uncertainties of the future. In the first interview she did not make any final decision. The worker's ability to identify with the child and to understand her feelings and put them into words had not only laid a basis for her own future relationship but had taken the immediate problem one step towards a solution.

Jean's last remark is an interesting one: 'You'd have to tell me off, wouldn't you?' This was obviously a half serious attempt to test out the worker in relation to any possible bad behaviour on her part. The worker's laughing reply: 'Certainly,' was I think the only one she could make, for it was impossible for her actually to sanction bad behaviour.

The next case record illustrates the way in which the child care worker can keep the home together and keep relationships alive for children, even though they are separated only temporarily, and shows the obvious need they have for this kind of help.

The three P. children—Doreen 6, Arthur 5 and Tommy 4 years of age—were placed in a Children's Home run by a voluntary society when their mother was admitted to hospital. They were expected to be in care for about a month, but their mother's stay in hospital was followed by convalescence and at the time of the interview they had been away from home for five weeks. The worker who saw them had had no previous contact with them as they had been placed in her area by a neighbouring authority.

When I called at the home I was ushered into a large waiting room with dark upright furniture. The nurse in charge told me that the children were very happy and had settled in with no trouble. They were brought to me one at a time from different parts of the building and as they came in I asked their names and exchanged a few odd remarks. After a few minutes the nurse left, leaving the children standing before me in a row, staring at the floor and looking uncomfortable. The nurse had been talking about an outing to the zoo which had happened the previous day, and for a few minutes we had a desultory conversation about the animals they had seen. Tommy said nothing at this point, and the other two spoke in a whisper and largely in mono-syllables. While we were talking, I got the children to fetch a couple of stools from the other side of the room and they settled down in a circle round me. This eased the tension to some extent.

The children had not met me before, and I knew nothing about them except that their mother was in hospital. I introduced myself and said I knew the lady who had arranged for them to come to the Home and she had asked me to call and see how they were getting on. I asked who had actually brought them here and Doreen said they had come in a lorry with mummy and daddy. I did not know what contact they had had with their own home since then so I asked if anyone had been to see them, they said no-one, so I added that at least I had come

K

now. I asked if they had heard from home at all and was told they had had a parcel at Easter.

I asked Doreen if she and Arthur had seen much of Tommy and she said 'No'. I said to Tommy: 'You feel rather lonely then I expect' and then asked if they had been together at all and Arthur told me that when they first arrived they had been in the Nursery with Tommy for a few days. At this point Tommy without any show of emotion said: 'I want to go home' (this was the first remark he had made). I said I expected he did, that everyone felt like that when they were away from home, and it must seem a long time to him. He said nothing. I asked them where their home was and Doreen said they lived in Badenham. I said I knew Badenham and it probably seemed to them to be a long way away. Tommy then said: 'I 'spect Badenham's in the pond.' I explained to him that because he had come away it did not mean that anything had happened to Badenham and that his home was still there waiting for him to go back to. It was evidently a great relief to him to talk about this and from being a silent spectator he began to monopolize the conversation. I suggested to him that he thought he might never be going back, and he told me of his fears in this respect and again said that he thought Badenham had gone away. The other two followed the conversation closely and I reminded Doreen that she had been away for a while before but had gone home again, saying that therefore she knew that she would be going back, but that Tommy, never having been away before could not feel sure about this.

We then talked about mummy going into hospital and I reassured them that she was getting better and that soon they would all go home.

I asked Tommy what he had had in the parcel from home, and explained that daddy had sent the parcel, and that it meant that daddy was thinking of him the way he thought about home. The others joined in and told me what they had received.

I asked them what things they had at home, and they all started to talk about their toys and what they did at home. As they talked the picture of home became more real to them, and they laughed and chatted to each other and to me. I think that to Tommy in particular the idea of home was becoming rather remote and it was noticeable how much more animated he became as, with the help of the others, he began to remember more and more about home and to talk about it. Altogether, I spent about an hour with the children, and when I left they asked when I would be coming again. I said I would do so in a few weeks but they would probably be at home by then. They went off quite happily, Tommy leaving the other two without trouble and looking much more confident.

Here we see the child care worker in action in rather difficult circumstances. Her friendly understanding but professional and un-emotional approach to the children gradually wins their confidence and creates an atmosphere in which they can talk. Her interpretation of their remarks in terms of their own fears helps them to express their anxieties openly. This reassures them and enables them gradually to reconstruct home again and the ability to do this gives still further reassurance. At no point does the worker force the issue. The main work of the interview is done by the children themselves and at the end of it they have had a complete experience.

Another casework technique which applies to work with children as well as adults is that of working from the positive factor in any situation to the negative rather than the reverse. For example, a child of 9 years who was well settled in a good foster home started stealing money to buy sweets to give to his foster mother. The worker's first remark to the child was, 'You are very fond of auntie, aren't you? And you want to show her that you love her and you want her to love you.' After this the worker went on to say that auntie liked to know the child loved her, but she didn't like the stealing, and nobody liked stealing. The same approach to the problem was made with the foster mother in this case, and to cut a long story short, this home was saved by the fact that the positive feelings behind the episode were recognized and worked on and brought into the open, so that they formed the basis for a new adjustment.

I would like to stress the absolute need there is for the children to be able to talk to the child care worker about their relationships and their fears and conflicts about the past, the present and the future. This involves a full discussion of all plans with the children them-selves. And it does not mean telling them about plans, but rather giving the children the time and opportunity to help in evolving the plan.

The child care worker's relationship to foster parents is a special one and unlike any other that we meet in casework. It is essentially a relationship of shared responsibility for the child, the foster mother being responsible for the day-to-day management and well-being of the child, and the worker taking the overall responsibility for enabling her to do this effectively. In the choosing of foster homes, therefore, it is important that the worker chooses people with whom she feels she can establish a good working relationship, because if they are insecure in their relation to her they are unlikely to stand the strain that the child will at times impose on them.

In interviews with prospective foster parents the worker's aim is, first of all, to help them to understand the nature of the work they are contemplating so that they can come to a decision about it based on a realistic consideration of all the factors involved and not merely on an emotional impulse. Secondly, while helping the foster parents to assess themselves in relation to the job, the worker's aim throughout the interview is to assess them herself.

A great deal has been said about the assessment of foster parents and their motives for doing the work. It seems to me that what we are trying to find is ordinary normal people with the average number of faults and failings. We are not looking for perfect parents because they only exist in theory and in the unconscious.

By 'normal' we really mean people who are not driven by guilt and anxiety but who are able to get something out of life and enjoy it, as well as contribute to it. Thus, the questions: 'What is it that these people get out of life? How do they get it? And in getting it how do they at the same time contribute?' are central ones for us. We want to get at the balance they have achieved between their negative and positive impulses. This can come out clearly in the interview as they talk abut their own family life in general and in relation to the foster child. They should also be asked about their own childhood and encouraged to talk about it as fully as possible because it will reveal their attitudes to their own parents and to life more clearly than anything else. The important thing to find out is what sort of people are these and how they have dealt with the experiences of life. How tolerant are they of themselves and others? Their attitude to what has happened to them is far more important than what actually did happen. I remember interviewing a prospective foster father who had been brought up in a large public assistance Home. When I asked him about life in the home he said: 'Well of course we missed our parents and nothing made up for that, but it wasn't too bad. The staff did their best for us but they were dreadfully overworked, and so we children had to help each other to get on as best we could.' All this was said without bitterness or resentment because somehow he had come to terms with what had happened. He was aware of what he had missed, but it had not prevented him from getting something positive out of the experience. He proved to be an excellent foster father although in theory one would have had serious doubts about him.

Our attempt to build up a picture of the prospective foster parents as people is a better method of assessment than a deliberate search for their unconscious motives in wanting a foster child, because the motive is part of a total pattern and cannot be understood or seen as a thing in itself. We must ask: 'How rigid is the pattern? Is it flexible enough to include a foster child?'

In the assessment interviews the worker will need to discuss the child's relationship with his own parents and the conflicts and problems that these will present both to him and to the foster parents themselves. The foster parents will need help to understand that difficulties which may arise (such as bedwetting, stealing, lying, etc.) are symptoms of the deprived child's natural urge to regress to dependence in any new environment which gives him hope. In other words the symptoms are inherent in the fostering situation—and will not be the foster mother's fault when they occur. While these discussions will do something to prepare the foster parents for events to come, they will not of course prevent an emotional reaction when the events actually occur; these we have to meet later on when the time comes. The discussion of these problems gives the child care worker the opportunity to put herself in the picture in relation to the work the foster mother is undertaking. She anticipates what may happen and is aware both of the difficulties and satisfaction of the work and will be available regularly to talk them over with the foster mother within the framework of shared responsibility

The actual role of the child care worker in relation to the foster parents is not easy to define, and I think we must say that it is a composite one—supportive, educational, and supervisory—with emphasis on each of the functions as need arises, but mostly with all three being carried out simultaneously. If the relationship becomes the worker-client relationship which we know in casework, something has gone wrong in our selection of the foster parents. We have then taken on a case not a working partner, and the work with the child will suffer in consequence.

The supportive role which is a passive one goes on all the time as part of the relationship. The supervisory role also is implicit in the relationship and is continuous, for we are always assessing the work and re-evaluating it in the light of new developments. The educational role is more active and positive. I should like to say a few things about this aspect of the work.

We are not attempting to give a professional education to foster parents. Such education would include a theoretical understanding of deprived children. We are really doing something more difficult and delicate—trying to help them in their personal adjustment to the child. The educational method we use is the casework technique of helping them to see what they are doing by putting their experience into words.

In this way they inform both themselves and us about the child. It is important for us to share with them the satisfactory experiences as well as the difficulties; for in times of stress we shall all need to remember them in order to see the total picture and the pattern of development as it emerges. It is impossible for the foster mother to see the total pattern when she is immersed in an emotional situation but we are always concerned with the pattern, and can help her to see something of it too. Foster parents (like parents) need continual reassurance about their positive feelings for a child as well as about their negative feelings. The guilt about having and loving someone else's child is ever present and may reveal itself in over-protectiveness and anxiety about health, and in an inability to discipline the child.

When the foster mother asks for direct advice about the handling of a child we shall need to apply our casework technique of talking out the problem rather than just giving an answer. Recently a child care worker was asked: 'What time do you think Mary [aged 9] should go to bed?' This seemed a simple seeking for information on a subject about which the foster mother was ignorant, as she had not previously had a child of this age in her care. But the worker had to consider how this information (if it were to be given) would be used. Would it be held as a threat over the child's head? Was the foster mother trying to put on to the worker the responsibility for disciplining the child? So she did not give the answer, but discussed bedtime problems in general and how one could tell when a child was getting enough sleep.

In her educational work with foster parents the child care worker helps the foster parents to objectify their experiences by talking about them and by seeing them in relation to a developing pattern. But there are times when she can do more. She can give the foster mother a new insight into a particular piece of behaviour. For example, a foster mother complained that her foster child (aged 7) would not leave her alone for a second. He was continually under her feet and in the way while she was in the kitchen trying to get her work done. The worker said: 'I think he's afraid of losing you and unless he can see you he can't be sure that you are still there. He's lost people before and he's determined not to lose you.' This foster mother was quite capable of understanding the situation especially as it was really a compliment to her. This same foster mother later told the worker about the child's enormous appetite. The worker said that many foster mothers found that this happened with children who had been deprived. When the foster father came in the foster mother said:

'Miss . . . says that children who have not had a happy home life always eat a lot'; then she added: 'I suppose they're making up for all the other things they haven't had.'

Sometimes the casework will centre round the foster mother's own feelings in relation to the child and not around the child's feelings or behaviour. For instance foster parents continually seek to explain adolescent behaviour in terms of bad heredity. The caseworker's only possible reply to that sort of statement is: 'Yes I can understand that you are much less sure of yourself with this child than you would be with one of your own.' If the worker falls into the trap of embarking on a discussion of heredity and environment she will not only entirely fail to convince the foster parents but will miss an opportunity of helping them.

Thus the work of interpreting and 'making sense' of what happens goes on. Naturally some people will understand more easily than others, but we often underestimate the foster parents' capacity in this direction, or we fail because we offer our own explanations and do not talk in terms of their own experience or in their language.

There is no doubt that some of the most difficult interviews that the child care worker has to conduct are with the parents of the children who are in care. The most strategic moment for the first contact to be made with the parents is when they apply for their children to be cared for. At this point every possible avenue can be explored to prevent the break-up of the family, and workers are realizing more and more the necessity for intensive and supportive casework to be done at this stage. Unfortunately in Great Britain our present legislation makes it difficult to do the kind of work needed before the children come into care, but we are gradually finding our way and there is no doubt that future development in the work will be along preventive lines.[1] Even if preventive work is not successful and the children have to be received into care this can be done as part of a plan for the whole future of the family with the co-operation of both children and parents.

In working with parents either before or after the children come into care, one of the things we shall be trying to assess is their capacity to make and maintain satisfactory relationships with their children. The main focus of our work will, therefore, be the parents' own problems, and if we are to help them at all our acceptance of them as they are is the first essential, as in all casework. This does not mean that we like or accept what they have done but that we see and under-

---

[1] This is now made possible by the Children and Young Persons' Act, 1963.

stand their point of view. So often a rejecting parent feels rejected and, in many cases, is actually rejected by the marriage partner (or the rejection may go back to earlier relationships). Our acceptance of the parents can be in itself a therapeutic experience for them, doing something to counteract feelings of rejection.

About two years ago a child care worker was called in to interview a young mother in a maternity hospital who was threatening that if she was made to leave the hospital with her baby she would kill him or herself. She had refused to feed the baby, handling him roughly and throwing him to the end of the bed. (She had repeatedly said: 'Why should I be expected to want my baby, when my mother never wanted me?') The worker had first interviewed the girl's husband who revealed the fact that she had entirely neglected their two-year-old child and that he, the father, had done everything for this child from birth. This had been possible because he was doing a residential job and they lived on the premises, but he was unable to manage the second child. He also explained that his wife felt very bitter because her own mother had not wanted her and she had been brought up in a children's Home.

In her interview with the mother at the hospital the worker did not argue or persuade her to keep her baby. Everybody else had taken that line with her and it had made her all the more determined to get rid of the child. She had become hardened and embittered by this approach. The worker simply said: 'I understand how you feel and that you are unable to want your baby because you feel your mother did not want you. I will therefore arrange to take the baby to a foster home for the time being. Perhaps later on you may want to see him and that will be possible.' The effect of this on the mother was to produce a flood of tears and the words: 'You are the only person who has understood how I feel.' Of course the mother did not immediately want her baby after this, and the child was in fact placed in a foster home and later adopted. But this acceptance and understanding of the mother was the beginning of the possibility of a change of attitude. One day she might have a child and want it.

In all cases where parents have failed to keep their children there is a tremendous sense of guilt which can be completely paralysing. They feel that however much they do they can never put right what they have done to their children. The result of this feeling is the apathy and depression we know so well or the projection of their feelings on to some external factor or person whom they feel to be to blame for what has happened. The sense of guilt and resulting hopelessness can be so great that they repudiate the relationship altogether and feel no sense of responsibility. This is one of the reasons why parents find it so difficult even to write a letter or send a parcel for the child's birthday. The mere act of putting pen to paper means that they have to think about the child to whom they write, and their guilt is so great that in an attempt to get rid of the guilt they get rid of the child, and so do not write. Thus the feeling of guilt is increased and a vicious circle is set up.

In our handling of interviews with parents we have to be careful not to increase their sense of guilt because this either puts them on the defensive or makes them reject the child still further by becoming more irresponsible about the relationship. In some cases it is not a good idea even to say 'the child misses you and wants to see you'. It is more of a relief for them to hear that he is settling down and getting on all right, because this means that they have not done him irreparable harm. Our visit in itself does a great deal to keep the child alive for them. As we talk about how he is and what he is doing they can gradually relate to him through us, provided that we have established a relationship with them by talking about their own problems and seeing them as people with a point of view and not as the bad parents. Often this means that we have to take on a parental role in relation to the parents for a time so that in building up a dependence on us and working through it they can come to tolerate their children's dependence on them. We can gradually enable them to see ways in which they can help us to help their child. They can begin to help by telling us all they can about the child, and the taking of a case history can be a valuable experience to the mother as well as of use to us.

The visiting of children should be talked about and planned with the parents. We must try to help them to see the point of view of the foster parents or houseparents who are caring for the child; their own jealousy about the child's love of foster parents will need to be brought into the open.

As I have already said, the parents of children in care are the most difficult group of people with whom we have to work in the child care services, and we have to face the fact that many of them are too emotionally immature and unstable to respond to the casework methods we have been discussing here. Many urgently need psychiatric treatment which we may be able to help them to obtain. Others may respond to the kind of help that the Family Service Units can give in England. But when all available methods of help have been considered we have to recognize that some parents will never be able to establish satisfactory relationships or a happy home life for their children. In these cases the only thing we can do is to help the children to establish stable and permanent relationships with foster parents, and to enable them as they grow up to come to terms with and tolerate their parents' illnesses and difficulties. This is a long and difficult task for the caseworker and for the child, and will demand the fullest use of casework skills and techniques.

11

ENFORCEMENT IN PROBATION CASEWORK*

A. W. HUNT

DEVELOPMENTS in social casework practice and training have been exceptionally pronounced in the last two decades, and of overriding importance in these developments has been the provision, mostly during professional training, of a rationale for casework practice. Emphasis has tended towards the insight-giving processes, acknowledgment of the individual's right to self-determination, and to the importance of a non-directive and accepting approach by the caseworker. Much contemporary literature and general teaching reflect experience in casework where need is overt or openly acknowledged by the subject, and in consequence a dilemma is presented to probation officers and others employed in the correctional field who are called upon to reconcile the concepts of generic casework teaching with the fact that they work in a clearly authoritarian setting in which many of their professional relationships contain the element of enforcement. The nature and implication of the dilemma are underlined in two recent contributions to our thinking on this subject made by Clare Winnicott in her article on 'Casework and Agency Function'[1] and Alan Roberton (1961), Governor of Hewell Grange Borstal Institution, in his paper on 'Casework in Borstal'.[2] Mrs Winnicott observes that 'When a child or an adult commits an offence of a certain degree and kind, he brings into action the machinery of the law. The probation officer who is then asked to do casework with the client feels he ought to apply techniques implying the casework principle of self-determination, but he loses everything if he forgets his relationship to his agency and the court, since symptoms of this kind of illness are unconsciously designed to bring authority

* Published in *The British Journal of Criminology*, Vol. IV, No. 3, January 1964.
[1] Published in *Case Conference*, Vol. VIII, No. 7, January 1962, pp. 178-84.
[2] Alan Roberton, 'Casework in Borstal,' *Prison Service Journal*, Vol. I, No. 2, pp. 15-22.

into the picture. The probation officer can humanize the machinery of the law but he cannot side-step it without missing the whole point of the symptom and the needs of the client.'[1] Alan Roberton also refers to the conflicting demands of the institutional setting, seen as a microcosm of society, and the needs of the boy. Attention is drawn to the desirability of maximum flexibility and adaptation to individual needs within the framework, but Mr Roberton concludes that 'to be casual or inconsistent about it or to take undue liberties with the framework would be unhelpful. Such inconsistency can only confuse the boy, may cause him to have some doubts about our general integrity and we may forfeit his respect.'[2]

Denial of the reality of the probation situation is often aided by the superficial fact that the probationer acknowledges need by virtue of the voluntary acceptance of a period of supervision, but there are few who would fail to recognize the naïvety of a suggestion that such an undertaking in itself implies recognition of need in any form. Moreover, there appears little doubt that, if the probation officer attempts to approach the probationer without careful reference to the fact that in many instances co-operation may be grudgingly given, he may not only fail to develop an approach which can honestly reconcile the fundamentals of casework with the approach necessary in many correctional settings, but he will also find his capacity to help a number of deprived and maladapted people seriously impaired.

A relationship which is enforced by the full sanction of the law is clearly open to abuse and it is recognized that the insights developed in relation to the motivation of the practitioner have been invaluable in pointing to the dangers of dominating and pontifical control. However, a cause for increasing concern over the years has been the frequency with which the probation officer's special position in relation to his probationers and others under supervision has been described in relatively negative terms. Experience shows that the negative aspects of enforcement have been referred to much more frequently than the positive elements, and many occasions have arisen when, because of uneasiness about the coercive factor in their relationships, probation officers have tried to deny the facts of the situation and have exaggerated the positive quality of their relationships to a highly unrealistic degree. It would seem that one of the most important reasons for such a situation rests on the fact that so much of our dynamic casework practice is based on psychotherapeutic techniques developed within

[1] op. cit.
[2] op. cit.

clinical settings where voluntary co-operation is assured and where such co-operation is deemed to be indispensable. Probation officers share with others the common experience of cases where a seriously disturbed person is considered unsuitable for treatment merely because he is not prepared to undertake treatment of his own volition or because of aggressive elements in the personality which conflict with special institutional or agency requirements. The basis of case selection of this type can be understood, but it is of very little assistance to the probation officer, many of whose cases would fall into such a category, and it would be a very great pity indeed if he concluded from such experience that lack of initial co-operation eliminated therapeutic opportunity or that maturation could not be encouraged.

With such problems as emotional disorder, personality defect or severe neurosis the relevance of the psychotherapeutic approach may be perceived. To see the relevance of such an approach is not easy when one deals with the many under-achieved, egocentric and extro-verted delinquents where the primary problem appears to be one of defective character development, or encounters professionally the range of spontaneous antisocial behaviour normally apparent in the growing child who has clearly not developed a pattern of delinquent behaviour.

The concept of delinquency as a neurotic manifestation has received considerable attention in recent years, but it does seem that this attention is disproportionate when a broad view is taken of criminality and antisocial behaviour as a whole. Personal experience of a wide range of delinquents suggests that much antisocial behaviour arises from the failure of a socialization process and that the compulsive, neurotic, affectionless or seriously unbalanced person is in the minority. Moreover, recognizable in much relatively casual delinquency is the presence of poorly sublimated aggression in which the failure of primary or social institutions of control is in evidence.

This reference to the aggressive element in behaviour is made, not from a limited definition, but from a wider and more fundamental view of the aggressive impulse in man as advanced by Anthony Storr in his article on the 'Psychology of Aggression'. For example, Dr Storr states that 'the aggressive impulse in man has a positive function which is vital to the independent life of the individual: and I hope I have also shown that aggression is a primary dynamic factor which cannot be eradicated. This is not to deny man's cruelty and hostility, but to point out that such behaviour is a distortion and a misdirection of independence, maturity and freedom. By far the majority of the human race is neither independent, nor mature, nor free: and therefore much human aggression is in the form of that destructive hostility which is associated with immaturity, insanity and restriction.'[1]

Such positive examination of a fundamental fact of the human psyche is helpful to probation officers not only because recognition of the creative potential of aggressive and assertive behaviour enables appropriate relationships to be formed, but also because it can point to the need for management features in treatment as distinct from the more sophisticated verbal processes.[2] In much recent literature concern with this and related themes may be identified and a fragmental view of opinion is most revealing.

The first paper to which reference is made is that of Dr Essex-Cater's report on his investigations during five years' experience in a remand home and in particular his observations on the mental health of the inmates. Dr Essex-Cater states that assessments of emotional reactions revealed 8 per cent who suffered severe emotional disturbance and were in need of active long-term psychiatric treatment, 42 per cent gave evidence of emotional disturbance requiring expert advice and in some cases short-term treatment, and 50 per cent of the boys were judged to be stable persons.[3] What is of interest in these evaluations is that in the assessment of stability reference was not made to delinquency as a manifestation of emotional disturbance, and it is acknowledged that separate criteria would have to be applied.

The second opinion of interest has been that contained in Melitta Schmideberg's address in June 1961, to the Third World Congress of Psychiatry in Montreal. Melitta Schmideberg was talking about the picture of New York's juvenile crime, and is reported as having described law enforcement and clinical treatment as 'blatant failures' and acknowledged that many serious juvenile criminals often came from apparently good homes. She was mainly concerned with the social causes of crime and indicted such factors as the prevailing over-permissive, child-centred upbringing which stressed needs rather than duties, lack of education and standards, sensationalism and sentimentalization of the sick offender, and recent belief in firm standards of right and wrong a outmoded and reactionary. Her criticism of law enforcement and social services appeared to be specific to the American

[1] A. Storr, 'The Psychology of Aggression,' *New Society*, London, Vol. I, No. 2, 1962.
[2] H. H. Allchin, 'Some Positive Aspects of Delinquent Behaviour,' *British Journal of Criminology*, London, Vol. III, No. 1, July 1962, pp. 38-46.
[3] A. Essex-Cater, 'Boys in Remand,' *British Journal of Criminology*, Vol. II, No. 2, Oct. 1961, pp. 132-48.

scene but she concluded that the 'permissive and non-punitive approach to the delinquent may have serious ill-effects.'[1]

Thirdly, attention is drawn to Reiner and Kaufman's recent publication *Character Disorders in Parents of Delinquents*. The authors refer to the treatment of such people by stating that their central aim is not to resolve unconscious conflicts but to further the maturation process. Such an aim is necessary because of 'primitive ego structure and because of the inability of such people to tolerate anxiety involved in self-examination. The analysis of their problems results either in flight or increased acting-out.'[2]

It is significant that someone like Melitta Schmideberg, with her psycho-analytic experience and orientation, talks so extensively about the social causation of crime and that Reiner and Kaufman talk about the therapist and client engaging 'not only in a process of unlearning faulty reaction patterns but also in a process of diversification and creation in social development'. My own reaction to such a proposition is that to be effective with many delinquents such treatment must occur in a relationship which is at least partially enforced. Before this view is expanded reference must be made to the contribution to the understanding of this problem made by D. W. Winnicott in his paper on 'The Anti-social Tendency'.[3] Dr Winnicott discusses the anti-social tendency rather than delinquency because the secondary social reactions in the latter made investigation difficult and because the tendency is apparent in the normal child when related to inherent developmental difficulties. The anti-social tendency is seen as being characterized by 'an element which compels the environment to be important', and Dr Winnicott says that it 'implies hope' and that 'management' is the appropriate treatment. When referring to typical trends of stealing and destructiveness in the anti-social tendency, he says of the second that 'the child is seeking the amount of environmental stability which will stand the strain of impulsive behaviour' and logically proposes that the 'nuisance value of the anti-social child is essential' and 'at best a favourable feature'.

The interpretation of the anti-social tendency is based on infantile phantasy need for control of aggressive impulses, and this is implicit in Dr Winnicott's observations on treatment, 'The treatment of the anti-social tendency is not psycho-analysis. It is the provision of child

[1] M. Schmideberg, Reported in Scott, 'The World Congress of Psychiatry,' *The British Journal of Criminology*, London, Vol. II, No. 2, Oct. 1961, pp. 177-81.
[2] B. S. Reiner and I. Kaufman, *Character Disorders in Parents of Delinquents*, Family Service Association of America, New York, 1961.
[3] D. W. Winnicott, *Collected Papers*, Tavistock Publications, London, 1958.

care which can be rediscovered by the child, and into which the child can experiment again with the id impulses, and which can be tested. It is the stability of the new environmental provisions which gives the therapeutics.'[1]

Unfortunately shortage of space does not allow discussion in greater detail of the implications of the preceding concepts, but there is little doubt that these concepts are indispensable to those working in the field of enforcement, and that they provide a theoretical link between dynamic psychology and the correctional field.

A rational development of a social or individual therapeutic approach in conditions of full enforcement has not yet matured, but there is convincing evidence to show that, contrary to the opinion of some clinicians, probationers and other offenders can make some adjustment even when compelled to relate to authority. In support of this view it is held that the most important and influential relationships in any person's life are those which are, in their very nature, enforced. A child is born into a family whether he or she likes it or not, and with very few exceptions there are no opportunities for the child to evade the necessity to make some adaptation to the demands made by the parents, and vice versa. Similarly in school, adjustment between child and teacher is necessary, even although in the first instance adjustment is unwillingly made. The elements of this process were graphically revealed in an incident in my recent experience. A boy aged 11 was asked by his probation officer what he felt about school. After some deliberation he replied, 'Oh, it's all right, but I 'ates it!' Anthony Storr is extremely interesting on this point and in *The Integrity of the Personality* he has this to say: 'In a régime in which rebellion is impossible since everything is tolerated, there is less scope for individual development than in one in which teachers as well as pupils have their rights. Loving a child does not mean always giving in to it, but does imply accepting the fact that rebelliousness and opposition are a necessary and valuable part of growing-up. Children need to fight with their parents, and for parents to refuse ever to fight back is to treat the child as less than a person and to fail to maintain a relationship with it. One way, therefore, in which the child's aggressive feelings may become dissociated and partially denied is for it to be faced with a parent who always gives in: another is for it to confront a parent who never does so.'[2]

In everyday life opportunities for withdrawal from trying situations

---

[1] ibid.
[2] Anthony Storr, *The Integration of the Personality*, Penguin edition, London, 1963, pp. 94-5.

are limited, and it seems that it is because of this fact that we develop our capacity to tolerate demands which ordinary living places upon us. For the majority of people with relatively normal personality and character development, marriage imposes similar disciplines; quarrels between husband and wife tend to resolve themselves much more rapidly because of the fact that opportunity to flee from an emotionally disturbing situation is not available, and because the fact of simple, urgent, sexual drive will force a compromise in order that straight-forward satisfactions may be achieved. Such adaptations are frequently made and often fail to occur in an atmosphere of quiet acceptance or forgiveness. Indeed, it would seem that in the developmental pattern of human beings concern is often expressed in vigorous and active terms and often in the guise of punishment. I would personally regard this as very important, because within our present sphere of practice the possibilities of active and positively expressed concern do not receive very much attention. Two recent examples taken from personal experience illustrate this particular point. A little girl, who is now aged six, was recently taken on a visit to some friends. During the course of this visit there was some discussion amongst the adults about children who had recently visited the house and who had created very considerable difficulty as a result of completely undisciplined and riotous behaviour. By all accounts no attempt had been made by the parents to control or guide the children in this situation. On returning home the girl asked why it was that the friend had been so critical of these children and why she had not liked them. She was told that this was probably because they had made such a nuisance of themselves and made life difficult for everyone else in the house. Her immediate reply to this information was, 'Well, why didn't their mummy and daddy get cross with them?'

The second example is the following letter from an 18-year-old Borstal boy to a probation officer known to him before committal:

'I am writing this letter to thank you for helping me out in court. I am sorry I have not written before, as I could not remember your name. I am hoping that when I come out of here that I will be under your supervision. I'm sorry if I seemed rude to you when we were outside of the court, but as you may already know, no-one could hardly expect me to be happy about going to court.

'Well, I am a grade two now and the board is tomorrow and I am hoping to get my threes with a bit of luck. If I do get them tomorrow I expect I shall be having my home leave somewhere around January,

L

which means I will have to report to you or whoever is going to be my probation officer.

'Please tell Mr S . . . if you see him that I'm sorry I let him down so much because I always did like him visiting my mother's house. And those little talks we had used to knock a bit of sense into me. Really what I needed when I was little was a good hiding but I always knew I would not get one, but this is just as good as one although it has taken me a long time to bring me to my senses.'

In neither of these cases does there appear to be a masochistic behaviour pattern.

Such examples are far from uncommon in work with delinquents, and from such incidents it may be concluded that lack of criticism or annoyance may be interpreted by the emotionally deprived as indicating a lack of basic concern and by the delinquent with weak ego as emasculated control. It is of significance that on many occasions an entirely unexpected response is encountered in a probationer or client who has become involved in further trouble. In spite of the fact that the probation officer does not feel resentful or annoyed, letters are received showing quite clearly that it is assumed that he will experience such feelings, and that such feelings will arise from basic feelings of regard and concern for the probationer. Again, in matrimonial conciliation, which is generally outside the terms of reference of this discussion, it is sometimes noticed that a couple who temporarily reconcile their differences and then separate will evade further contact with the probation officer because it is assumed that such a break in marriage will produce disappointment in him. Such expectations do not arise from the facts of the situation at all, but quite clearly from the expectation of behaviour, based on the role he fills. It is vitally necessary that these facts of phantasy and behaviour should be fully taken into account, by recognizing a need which has to be satisfied, without at the same time playing into phantasies of some people who anticipate vindictive and revengeful responses. It goes without saying that if this is to be done the fullest possible account must be taken of the developmental influences which are brought to bear on each individual person and the type of feelings which such experiences have stimulated and reinforced.

Before referring to ways in which probation casework techniques should acknowledge the special needs of the probation setting, it is necessary to return briefly to one other consideration arising from the original observations about enforcement in primary social situations.

In everyday life anxiety may express itself in simple ways, such as in procrastination and evasion, but within the ambit of the court these features are encountered more frequently and in such degree that people are found who are prevented from taking even the most simple step which might remedy the source and cause of anxiety. Given a chance, most people will tend to take the superficially easy way out of their difficulties, and it is only when they are faced with a situation from which they cannot extricate themselves, or faced with a person they cannot avoid, that they are helped to overcome inertia sometimes produced by quite intense anxiety. This, it is felt, is one of the special strengths of the enforced relationship, and it can be seen why it is that probation officers are often the recipients of information which could more appropriately be disclosed, for example, to a psychiatrist or family doctor. The following example is used to illustrate the argument. A short time ago a probation officer completed supervision of a boy in his early teens whose behaviour was being adversely affected by excessively indulgent and over-protective handling by the mother. He was petulant and selfish and his thefts were not of a compulsive nature but more of the 'what I want I have' variety. Initially the child guidance clinic had offered some assistance, but no treatment was possible because the mother repeatedly failed to keep the appointments. During the course of supervision it became increasingly obvious that the mother's attitude towards her son was coloured by feelings previously experienced in a very uneasy and ambivalent relationship with her younger brother. Her brother had, long before the boy's behaviour became increasingly troublesome at home, died tragically as the result of a rapid malignant illness. It appeared, and was subsequently admitted by the mother, that she felt very guilty for the many real and imagined unkindnesses shown to her brother, and her indulgent handling of her son was related to her need to make reparation in some way for her past hostility. By the end of supervision the mother was accustomed to talk quite freely about these considerable anxieties, the nature of which she had previously kept secret. On her own admission, she benefited from these interviews, but when it was suggested to her that, even although official contact would have ended, she could call and see the probation officer at his office, which was quite close to the home, she found this quite impossible to do. Her superficial reason was simply that if she came to see him he might think her reason for anxiety silly, and she would have difficulty in explaining her presence. If the probation officer called on her, however, under the provision of an Order which made it necessary for him to see her and her to see him, then the matters which caused her anxiety could be touched upon in the general course of interview. However, it seemed equally implicit that the fact of enforcement provided reassurance for the mother that relationship was finite and that the demands she made could be contained by this situation.

Probation casework is rich in examples showing how people may be helped in an enforced situation and how even the very dull are able to perceive the positive implications which may in the first instance appear to be against their interests. Simple examples can illustrate the point.

The first case is of a young man in his early twenties who had drifted away from what was a relatively settled home, but one in which control and guidance were limited. During his independent life he encountered difficulties over employment, found himself in financial trouble and committed what was a relatively simple offence to solve his immediate problem. The early phases of supervision were marked by a general air of discouragement which did not amount to seriously morbid depression, and the young man was becoming deterred from energetic pursuit of necessary employment because of very real difficulties due to some prevailing unemployment. The probation officer concerned took practical and active measures to secure employment for this young man and they spent many hours together in this search. At one stage shortly before it proved fruitful the probationer was seen in the absence of his officer by a colleague. This colleague was surprised to encounter very positive warmth after what was a short period of supervision, and after some difficulty in describing the quality of his relationship the probationer eventually said, 'I wish my father had been like Mr Blank because when I am with him he makes me feel that things are going to get better for me at last.' Although a simple example it shows how much reassurance can be given by the competent management of the situation by a caseworker, and obvious parallels can be seen between this type of situation and the type of encouragement and reassurance which is given to children by the untroubled action of parents.

The second example is of a boy in his very early teens who is attending the play group run by some probation officers as an adjunct to their normal, individual casework. The boy concerned is an only child, and the outstanding characteristic of his upbringing was that he had been indulged, and characteristically he was suspicious of the motives of his indulgent parents and displayed some obvious signs of insecurity. In the early stages of his attendance in the group his behaviour was not openly destructive but he contrived to annoy the other children who were working or playing happily together, and such disturbances occurred almost invariably when his own probation officer was absorbed with some of the other children. This covert destructiveness was having a detrimental effect on the group as a whole and it ultimately became necessary to apply the sanction of withdrawing the boy from the group. He was given the reason for this by his probation officer who made some simple interpretation of the anxieties behind the boy's behaviour, and accompanied this by a reasonable explanation of the way in which he allocated his time. The boy displayed signs that he was anxious to continue attending and the week following his exclusion he presented himself at the office. He was again seen by his probation officer who verbally anticipated certain behaviour. The boy re-entered the group, and it was noticeable that henceforth the boy made some adjustment to this simple social situation, and in the following attendances there was a marked reduction in the mischievously destructive behaviour.

The last of the examples concerns a man in his middle thirties who had a long record and was placed on probation with certain knowledge that failure would result in a long prison sentence. It was evident that the fear of such a sentence acted as an additional external discipline and the man succeeded in keeping free from actual criminal behaviour. However, he broke contact after taking some seasonal employment and the probation officer recognized the set of circumstances which had preceded earlier criminal behaviour. A warrant was issued, the man was arrested and was eventually brought before the original sentencing court. In his behaviour towards the probation officer the man showed little obvious resentment and appeared to acknowlege and accept the reason given for the action taken. During the period of remand the man received news that attempts had been made to retain his employment for him and he saw that the report on his conduct was without obvious bias. A fresh Order was made, but for several days it was not possible for the probationer to commence residential employment. The probation officer shared with him the difficulties of finding temporary accommodation and it was noticeable that the officer was asked repeatedly not to 'worry' about the man. Subsequent discussion with this man at a much later date revealed that he had been impressed by a feeling that his further criminal behavior and his material circumstances were of direct personal concern to the probation officer, and this theme emerged repeatedly during a phase of supervision lasting some eighteen months.

The examples given are quite ordinary ones but they are representative and valuable in providing a focus for some general conclusions.

L*

1. Probation is inescapably identified with punishment as well as reform and reclamation. If emphasis is given to the deterrent and revengeful element then this must create difficulties for the caseworker who is motivated by reparative feeling. If, however, it is seen that there are directly positive features of punishment, notably an explicit expression of concern for the offender, it is possible to draw on experience of primary family and social situations to provide a conceptual basis for casework activity.

2. Some external control of the individual can assist in the process of maturation because it provides real and promised stability, and again by implication can contain the unconscious and sometimes near-conscious anxieties about aggressive and destructive impulse.

3. Enforcement goes some way to counter superficial evasion and avoidance behaviour which prevents appropriate social action on the part of the individual.

4. The enforced relationship and casework are not mutually exclusive. Indeed, in many respects the probation casework process is enriched by enforcement, and the explanation appears to centre on the fact that enforcement is an essential component of all early socializing processes. If there is anything distinctive about casework in enforcement, it is that the caseworker needs more often to show himself as concerned through positive action, even although it is found that such activity does not prevent the coincidental use of interpretive techniques or the relatively inactive processes of casework in the clinical setting.

12

WORKER-CLIENT AUTHORITY
RELATIONSHIPS IN SOCIAL WORK*

ELLIOT STUDT

A FRAMEWORK for study of the social worker's authority towards the client was not necessary when the profession was saying that case-work could not be 'done' from an authority position. Nor was it pressing so long as authority was considered to be a factor in only one kind of service, i.e. corrections, or in only a few special situations, the 'authoritative settings'. But recently the profession has been noting that all social workers use authority in some way or other. The public welfare worker acts with authority when he determines eligibility; the group worker uses authority in refusing to permit certain behaviour in the clubroom; the child welfare worker is authoritative in selecting a foster home; the school social worker represents the authority of the state in insisting with child and family that he must attend school; the therapist in the clinic exercises authority in setting the conditions for treatment. While we recognize that there is a commonness in all these actions, we are not sure it is in reality the same thing for a family worker to say to a voluntary client, 'This is the way we will work together', as it is for a probation officer to say to an offender, 'There are certain things you cannot do. If you do them we will have to report back to the court'. If it is true that authority appears in all helping relationships, then we should agree about what authority is. We need also to understand its dynamics in action and how its exercise varies from setting to setting.

In all the examples of authority actions by social workers towards clients listed in the preceding paragraph, the social worker is engaged in defining certain aspects of the client role which must be accepted by the client if he is to participate in the service. Our task in this paper is to propose a framework for examination of such actions. First let

* Published in *Social Work*, New York, Vol. IV, No. 1, January 1959.

us look at the nature of authority in general and the social conditions which create authority relationships.

Authority appears as a relationship between persons only in an organization of human beings to accomplish a task. Authority is not the power of a bully to control the actions of a weaker person, since authority is always legitimized power. It is not the influence of one friend over the decisions of another, since authority is a special form of influence occurring only when one person has certain official responsibilities towards the behaviour of another. Rather, authority is created when, in order to get the job done properly, a person in one position in an organization is authorized to direct the role activities of a person in another position.

In using this definition of authority we should note that the authority of one person towards another does not extend beyond the responsibilities of the relationship between the two positions. The 'directing' referred to should be understood in the sense of 'giving direction to'. It calls for relatively few authority actions as such and depends for effectiveness in large measure on other forms of influence. Most authority actions are simply a matter of making explicit, in a particular behavioural context, the role definitions governing the subordinate position.

The positions to which authority is delegated are links in a hierarchical chain of relationships in task-oriented social organizations. These chains of relationship connect broad social authorization of the task with the activities of the person at the bottom who is doing a primary unit of the task. We can think of the operation of these chains of relationships as the sanctioning process by which authority actions at each intermediate position are directed, limited and made socially responsible.

The sanctioning of authority involves both the delegation of responsibility for certain decisions and actions to each position in the chain and the acceptance of the rightfulness of the authority by the persons towards whom it is exercised. The dynamics of authority actions can only be understood by keeping in mind the essential two-way process of delegation and acceptance by which authority is sanctioned.

The length and complexity of the chain of relationships which implement this sanctioning process vary greatly among human organizations depending on the nature of the social task to be accomplished. Because the family is the basic unit in our society for the socialization of children, there are few formal steps (such as legal marriage) in-

serted between the community's authorization of parental responsibilities in the basic law and the authority actions of the particular
parent. On the other hand, when the political unit has taken responsibility for meeting economic need, many complex links appear in
the sanctioning system by which the authorization of federal funds for
public assistance is translated into action towards an individual
applicant in the local welfare office. Still another form of sanctioning
organization is observed in provisions for medical services in our
society, with two sanctioning systems—the professional and the
legal—operating jointly to authorize an individual doctor to practise
medicine.

When one examines the positions to be filled in a given sanctioning system, one observes that all of them are assigned certain responsibilities in relation to the total task. Certain of these positions are
filled by persons who contribute to the task by influencing the activities
of others. Persons in the positions at the bottom of the chain of
sanctioning relationships do not discharge their responsibilities
through other people but are assigned units of the basic task in relation
to which they make decisions and take action. It is at this final level
that the basic task of the organization is achieved.[1]

In a factory this final unit of responsibility consists of the materials
and tools which the individual manages in order to produce his
share of the product. In such an organization all the personnel required
to achieve the task are employed and the organization owns the
product of their work. There is, however, a different pattern of
relationships in those change-producing social organizations which
are responsible for developing, educating, socializing, and helping
people. The product of these organizations is a kind of human functioning whose benefits accrue to the people involved and to the
community at large. The basic work of such tasks is not done by
those who are employed by the organization but by those who are
being helped or educated. Thus the child in school is the one who
does the learning which is the goal of the educational institution,
while the teacher contributes to this task by guiding the child in his
role as student. Similarly in the social agencies, it is not the social
worker who does the basic task for which the organization is created.
It is the client who gets well, achieves rehabilitation, maximizes his
functioning, and makes constructive use of resources or the goal of

---

[1] I am indebted to Elliot Jacques, *The Changing Culture of the Factory*, The Dryden
Press, Inc., New York, 1952, pp. 249-97, for several concepts in this analysis of authority
actions.

the service is not achieved. This fact points to a significant characteristic of the social agency as a change-producing organization.
For such organizations the basic task is achieved through the operation of persons in a role group who are never employed by the agency
but who become members of the organization for shorter or longer
periods of time in order to benefit from participation in the agency's
task. Each client has a position in the organization during his period
of need This position passes through phases from intake to termina-
tion as the client moves towards the goal of more independent functioning. Thus the client of a social agency temporarily becomes a
functioning member of the social organization and, while he is a
client, is subject to its sanctioning system and participates in its
authority relationships. To the social worker is delegated the authority
to direct the client's role behaviour through its various phases so
that the goal for which he and the organization came together can
be achieved.

If such a definition of authority is to be useful in understanding
authority relationships in social work, we should be able to observe
the central concepts of the definition in reality situations. According
to our definition any given authority event would reveal a social
organization, two related positions, and two persons in the positions
which are interacting to produce a particular outcome. Let us look
at a simple authority action to see if our conceptual formulation
is adequate and illuminating in the effort to understand practical
reality.

The authority event used below as an example is not a social worker-
client authority action, but is drawn from a change-producing
organization. It has more than one kind of usefulness for our purposes: it is somewhat more simple than a social worker-client action;
and since it is based in an institution it is easier to perceive the client
as 'a member of the organization'. Furthermore, since this is a strict
authority situation, it is useful for examining the question of latitude
for choice among actions as the authority structure becomes more
specific in its definition. As we analyse this action, we should take
care to be sure that social organization, two positions, and two
persons can actually be observed interacting. If they are all here,
then we will have to take each of these concepts into account in any
further analysis.

The scene is a young men's reformatory and the action takes place in
a mess hall, where the men are lining up with trays along a counter.

As reported to the interviewer by one of the inmates, the action went this way: 'I nearly got a discipline charge last week. I felt I was going to blow up. I had to take it out on something and I didn't want to get into a fight. I tried to steal an extra piece of cake as I went through the line. Luckily the officer who saw me knew me. He told me to put it back and passed it off as a joke.'

Let us look first at the authorizing social organization and the particular authority position. This is a reformatory with a treatment orientation. In the generalized groups occupied by persons in this institution we note that two reciprocal roles have been established —that of officer and that of inmate—each with rather clearly out-lined rights, duties, and obligations towards the other. The particular position which we are noting—in which any of a number of officers might have been stationed—is that of a mess hall supervisor with general responsibility for assuring a fair distribution of food to all inmates. Some of the means by which the responsibility of this position is to be discharged have been specified, while others are permitted and still others are proscribed. Thus the mess hall super-visor may give a discipline charge to a rule violator but he is forbidden to hit him. In the verbal realm he has wide latitude for pos-sible action all the way from a stern rebuke to letting the incident go without comment. The general expectations of the sanctioning social organization as to what is acceptable performance in this position clearly affects the outcome of this authority action. For instance, the outcome would have been different if administration required that a discipline charge be written for every such rule viola-tion; or if the officer perceived administration as rewarding officers who sent in many such charges; and still different if inmate and officer had learned from experience that administration did not back up its officers when such charges were written.

Even in this quite strictly defined authority position we note the decisions which were made by the particular officer who took part in the action, and how much he contributed to the final outcome. The officer might have chosen to discharge his responsibility by giving a provocatively hostile rebuke which could have triggered off the explosion which the inmate was trying to control. If, on the other hand, the officer had chosen to let the incident go by without com-ment he might unwittingly have confirmed in the inmate a pattern of using this means for the outlet of aggression. What the officer did choose to do was bring the violation to the inmate's attention in a pleasant fashion. The action he chose limited the area in which the young man could discharge his explosive feelings, both by making it impossible to steal cake and by refusing to let this incident become a focus for all the inmate's wrath against authority.

The position in which the inmate was operating is more complicated and difficult to describe. In the first place, the organization has defined for him a generalized role—that of inmate—which is pervasive throughout the activities of his life in the institution. The expectations of the inmate role emphasize conforming behaviour towards a number of persons, each of whom is in a somewhat different supervisory position over him. At the same time by reason of his role, he is also a member of an inmate population. The culture of this population brings pressure to bear on him for conforming to values which are contrary to the expectations of the organization. When the inmate gets caught in the group in an effort to defeat institutional rules, the incident is crucial for his relationship with the organization and with his peers and is particularly difficult for him when the officer acts in a contemptuous or essentially debasing fashion. Thus the role of inmate is an inherently conflictual one and behaviour in any given episode will be affected by the interplay of antagonistic expectations.

Finally, the outcome of this particular authority action was also affected by the person in the inmate role. He was a person who was chronically sensitive to authority actions and particularly so at this moment. However, in spite of his sense of imminent explosion from within, he was able to accept the action of the officer and be influenced by it, perhaps because of some sense that the officer viewed him as an individual. Another person in his state of mind might by his general attitude have so affected the officer's behaviour that there would have been the kind of rebuke which triggers explosive action.

It is evident from this example that we will need to examine the social organization in which the authority action occurs, the two positions which are related by authority, and the two persons in these positions in order to understand what goes on in any given authority event. Let us see what we know in general about these components of an authority relationship in social work. In this examination we should be ready for the possible emergence of another essential concept, since social work operation is more complex than the example we have just analysed.

The organization of any agency reflects the social task for which it is responsible. The task of the service agency employing social workers is that of meeting crucial needs in the lives of individual human beings, needs which are of high enough incidence in a given society to require organization to meet them. This is a task area of marked social and personal sensitivity. It impinges deeply on the values which govern the interrelationships of people—affecting homes, happiness, welfare and integrity. Since persons in serious need are also sometimes socially dangerous, protection of the community as well as of the individual sometimes becomes an explicit part of the task. Furthermore, the magnitude of the task, when many individuals in a society experience needs that can only be met through social organization, calls for extensive mobilization of financial resources and professional personnel.

Given a social task which includes meeting widely experienced individual needs, protecting the community, and supporting values, we can expect to find in the social services a complex organization involving a number of sanctioning systems. Each of these systems is required to provide certain resources in money or skills and to implement the support of certain values. At least three sanctioning systems operate simultaneously in the organization of the social services: the legal which establishes the basic structure of services and rights; the administrative which is responsible for getting the job done; and the professional which is concerned with competence and values. Some services are also responsible to a fourth sanctioning system, the religious, by which certain additional values are protected. Each of these systems has its characteristic decision-making patterns, governing values and reference groups. All of them affect the design of the social worker's authority position, and set up certain expectations about performance in it.

These sanctioning systems are organizationally related to each other in different ways in different service agencies, depending on the particular social need to be met by the agency. For instance, a private family agency with its voluntary case load is governed, relatively remotely, by the legal system through a legislative act authorizing incorporation for certain purposes. In this sort of agency the professional and administrative systems have tended to become identical so there is minimal complication and little cross-checking by various sanctioning systems. Compare this with the field of mental health where the case load includes a wide range of voluntary and involuntary clients. In this field several professions together take responsibility for the service with ultimate authority in both the administrative and professional systems lodged in the medical profession. Also in this field the legal sanctioning system is more active, licensing medical practitioners, establishing certain public services, and making decisions about those clients who must be hospitalized involuntarily. Then compare either of these fields with that of corrections where all clients have demonstrated some potentiality for danger to society. In this field, the legal sanctioning system makes decisions about every client; all the professions (each of which is sanctioned by its characteristic system) are involved in service; and administrative processes have certain responsibilities such as custody which, though often organizationally separated from treatment, affect the professional processes.

One way of understanding differences among fields of social service is to observe the interrelations of sanctioning systems which are deemed necessary to authorize the activities of each service. It seems evident that the greater the authority of the agency to act in relation to involuntary clients, and the more serious the potential danger to society from client behaviour, the more complex is the organization of the sanctioning systems required to provide the necessary resources and to protect the values affected by the service.

An important result of the fact that there are several sanctioning systems in social work organization is the emergence of the decision-making team as a significant step in the exercise of social work authority. This is the additional concept which we anticipated. Most social services are provided through the joint operation of a number of personnel each of whom may represent a different sanctioning system. These personnel may be stationed in the same agency with the worker; or may represent other agencies necessary to the service required by the particular case. Each member of this decision-making team (of which the clinical team is only one example) has a differently defined responsibility, yet the areas of responsibility overlap; and the service which ultimately gets to the client in the one-to-one or one-to-group relationship is affected by the shared decision-making of this team. The way the social worker's role is defined within this team affects the nature of the decisions which will be reached in its deliberations; and these decisions limit and direct the social worker's exercise of authority in decision-making with the client. The more complex the organization of sanctioning systems necessary for giving the particular service, the more complex will be the authority relationships in the team, and the more probable that difficulties at this point will have an unfortunate effect on the worker's use of authority with the client.

The social worker's authority position is an individualizing link between the social resources provided by the organization and the client with his needs. Therefore, it would be useful at this point to modify the order of our outline and examine the necessities of the client's position as he enters into membership in the service organization before we look at the authority position of the social worker.

One of the significant characteristics of the client group is its vulnerability to the exercise of authority. Individuals would not be clients if they were not at least temporarily handicapped in taking responsibility for some aspect of their personal lives.[1] In such situations they are particularly dependent on the authority person who can link them to the social and psychological resources which are necessary to repair damage and to reinstate their ability to manage for themselves. They are impelled to seek help because of internal or external difficulties which matter to them, and the resources to which they can turn are usually limited. In this perspective social work tends to deal with a 'captive case load', and the opportunities for well-intentioned misuse of this power position are numerous.

In a democratic society we can expect to find certain important safeguards built into the processes which authorize intervention by authority persons in such vulnerable lives. Some of these are built into the definition of the client position. The stipulation that the request for help shall be voluntary is one of these. The professional emphasis on the client's right to self-determination within the limits of reality is another. In certain services we find legal protections for the rights of clients such as provisions that financial assistance shall be granted when eligibility is demonstrated, and procedures for appeal from disadvantageous decisions. Social concern that the persons in authority towards needy people shall have been tested and tried through an educational process which ensures their trustworthiness for this responsibility also stems from recognition of the vulnerability of persons in the client role. Another characteristic of the group of persons who appear in the client role is the very wide variation among clients in ability to take responsibility for themselves. Some have the strengths necessary for self-management in all essential areas. Some are limited in their ability for independent management in only one area. There are others, however, who are not only seriously limited in ability to take responsibility for themselves but are also

[1] This formulation does not sufficiently take into account the nature of need brought by members of many groups served by group workers. This whole statement is in process of formulation and presents a number of theoretical problems requiring further testing against the realities of various kinds of social work practice.

socially dangerous and unwilling to seek help in modifying their situations. Some, found particularly in correctional case loads, are supported by their group relationships in a strong antagonism to any intervention which would modify their social functioning.

As a result of these facts about persons in client positions one would expect to find in the social services a graded series of definitions of the client role which reflects the different abilities of individuals to take responsibility for themselves. At one end of the range the client position is designed to allow for self-determination in all areas of personal functioning. Such positions are usually found in private family agencies and in outpatient psychiatric clinics. There are intermediate positions in which the role definition of client calls for submitting one or more aspects of personal functioning to shared decision-making with the worker, such as the economic area in public assistance, parent-child communication in foster home care, and the management of illness in the medical services. At the other end of the range would be positions for clients who enter the role involuntarily and are assigned to work with authority persons in relation to extended areas of personal functioning. Such positions are found in agencies dealing with parental neglect, in many institutions, and in correctional services. All social agency case loads fit within this continuum, with variously designed positions for clients which reflect the nature of the need, the ability of the client to take responsibility for his own life, and the potential danger to society in his behaviour.

Finally, client motivation to accept and use authority constructively in the accomplishment of life tasks varies over a wide range. Our concern as a profession that the request for help be voluntary stems in part from the fact that such a request is an explicit sanction from the client for the worker's use of authority. Yet there are many client situations where the combined needs of the individual and his community require social work services even when the client is not able or willing to make a verbal request for help. We have seen that authority does not become effective except as the person towards whom it is exercised sanctions its use and acts in accord with the intention of the authority person. The profession must therefore be concerned with the possibility of motivating involuntary clients to make constructive use of authority relationship; and with the skills by which this is accomplished. In accepting such a responsibility we will continue to give attention to the safeguards which prevent the use of extended authority except as individual and social need warrant such intervention and the proper authorization has been made.

We have said that authority appears as an aspect of human relationships in social organizations where a person in one position is responsible for directing the role performance of a person in another position. Under this definition the social worker's position carries authority for directing the client's use of his position in the organization towards the achievement of the goals for which client and service come together. The authority allocated to the worker's position will be restricted or extended depending on the kind of responsibility assumed by his agency for the personal functioning of the client. At the same time the social worker's authority will be delimited by the operation of the decision-making team with which he shares responsibility for the service. Thus in one sense the worker's position seems to be that of a middle man in the authority system. He brings information to the decision-making team, participates in its deliberations, and administers decisions made at this organizational level. In work with the client he encourages the client in making his own decisions.

It is important, however, not to ignore the decisions which the social worker makes independently as he chooses among the alternative behaviours possible to him. There is in fact an extremely wide latitude of decision-making which is necessarily left in the hands of the social worker as he deals with clients, whether he is determining the number and frequency of interviews, establishing eligibility, selecting a foster home, or evaluating a violation of probation. No matter how stringent and detailed the authority structure within which the worker operates, his primary assignment is to individualize the provisions by which the social service is given. In the most strict authority structure, therefore, he has authority to select among the available alternatives in terms of the individual with whom he is working. Such decisions are often made at the moment of action and are based on information to which only he has access. In this activity the worker has at his disposal a wide range of means by which one person may influence another; in addition, what he does with the client is relatively unobserved.[1] In the light of these facts about his function, the authority position of the social worker is necessarily designed to allow for flexible exercise of extensive power to influence others while ensuring responsible action governed by the purposes of the service and the needs of the clients.

One of the attributes of the person in authority which significantly

[1] Lloyd E. Ohlin, 'Conformity in American Society Today,' *Social Work*, Vol. 3, No. 2 (April 1958), pp. 60-1.

affects the outcome of authority actions is the way he feels about his position. Elliot Jacques has pointed out that the person in the authority position also sanctions his exercise of authority when he is clear about what is required of him, competent to undertake the task, and able to resolve the ambivalences which are stimulated by the exercise of authority.[1] When the person in authority is uneasy about his assignment, he tends to take refuge in abdication from or over-assertion of the authority for which he is legitimately responsible. Either of these adjustments interferes with his effectiveness in the total task. Since the social work profession has in general been uncertain about the place of authority in the dynamics of helping, it can be expected that many practitioners experience uneasiness in social work positions which call for an extended use of authority.[2]

It is clear the positions in which this amount of power to influence the lives of others is sanctioned should be filled with persons who can make these decisions competently and in the interest of the client. Such positions call for mature, disciplined workers who are capable of relatively independent functioning. They need the realistic knowledge of life and the personal strength necessary to make decisions, to exercise authority responsibly, and to stand as toughly flexible members of the decision-making team. They also need educational preparation for analysing and understanding the dynamics of authority in the total social work task.

Thus it would seem that authority relationships between social workers and clients are determined by the following facts:

Social workers and clients come together in a complex *organizational setting* in which a number of sanctioning systems combine to define the task and determine the allocation of authority.

Social workers act as members of *decision-making teams* whose decisions both limit and direct the social worker's exercise of authority with the client.

The *authority positions* in which social workers are placed require ability to share decisions at the team level; independent functioning at the level of primary responsibility; and ability to free the client for self-determination to the extent of his ability within the definition of his position.

The *positions for clients* are variously designed within the different social services, depending on variations among groups of clients in

---

[1] Jacques, op. cit., pp. 275-91.
[2] Lloyd E. Ohlin, Herman Piven, and Donnell M. Pappenfort, 'Major Dilemmas of the Social Worker in Probation and Parole,' in Herman D. Stein and Richard A. Cloward, eds., *Social Perspectives on Behavior* (Glencoe, Ill., The Free Press, 1958), pp. 251-62.

ability to use help responsibly. The authority of the worker is restricted or extended depending on the extent to which the personal life of the client is drawn within the definition of his position as client in that particular service.

The *persons in the client positions* vary extensively in their ability to use authority constructively. Since effective exercise of authority depends on its sanction and use by the person in the subordinate position, social workers are often faced with the necessity of helping individual clients relate positively to the authority which directs their role performance in the service.

The social worker as the *person in the authority position* needs to be clear as to the nature of the authority which is delegated to him, flexible in authority relations at the different levels of decision-making, and skilful in handling destructive responses to authority from the client.

It would be useful to test this general description of authority relationships between social workers and clients in a number of different ways. On the one hand, it would be theoretically valuable to examine a number of different samples of social work practice to see how differences in social organization, in the design of worker and client positions, and in the persons who fill these positions are reflected in differences in the exercise of authority. What, for instance, are the professional problems and skills in the use of authority by the group worker, the public assistance worker, the caseworker in the child guidance clinic, the institutional caseworker, and the probation officer? What is the base which is common to all? What are the different emphases which flow from different structural provisions and orientations?

On the other hand, this outline could be useful in locating the source of problems in authority relations appearing in a particular service. Are the expectations of the organization clear or conflicting? Does the decision-making team operate effectively? Is the worker sure of the nature of his authority? What of the client position— does it harbour unsuspected conflicts? What steps are taken to motivate clients to participate usefully in authority relationships?

Of the many questions which require further exploration, three occur to the writer as particularly significant for problems of practice.

1. *Authority relationship and action*

Professional use of an authority relationship for helping requires a careful distinction between authority relationship and authority action.[1] Not all actions of an authority person towards the person in the subordinate role are authority actions. The person in any authority position also uses many other means of influence, such as counsel, exploration of possibilities, supportive understanding, and training in skills. However, there tends to be a halo effect from an authority relationship which can lead the subordinate to perceive all actions of the authority person as authority actions.

We have long known that professional control of the helping process can be achieved through awareness of the psychological and social forces which enter into the helping relationship. If authority is a real factor in social worker-client relationships, lack of attention to its operation could well result in a more diffuse and rigidly determining authority influence than is warranted by the facts or desirable for the client's freedom to act in his own behalf. It seems probable that clarification by the worker for himself and with the client as to the authority which is actually delegated to the worker's position can help to reduce the halo effect and limit the inappropriate or unaware use of authority by both worker and client.

Although increased awareness of the dynamics of authority in relationships can help to reduce undesirable effects of authority actions on helping, we still need more exploration about what happens to the helping relationship as the worker's responsibility for authority actions increases. As a profession we have been fearful that each increment of authority reduces the ability of the client to use the relationship for help. On the other hand, social workers in a number of services have reported that appropriate authority actions actually enhance the ability of the client to take responsibility for himself. It may well be that one of the major skills in the use of authority in helping involves the gradual substitution of other means of influence for the authority actions which are necessary in the initial phase of the relationship. Only further study of actual authority actions in the context of the helping relationships can resolve these questions.

2. Design of worker-client positions

It is evident that these two positions are reciprocal in that a change in one implies a change in the other; therefore it is useful to consider them together as a certain kind of role relationship. This role model has been primarily drawn from experience in those services where the client makes a voluntary request for help and retains responsibility

[1] Herbert A. Simon, *Administrative Behavior* (The Macmillan Co., New York, 1957), pp. 125-8.

for all his life decisions. The authority of the worker in this model tends to be limited to the decisions which he makes in managing the helping process.

As we have given increased attention to social work positions in which the worker takes more initiative in motivating clients to want help and increased responsibility for decisions in the client's personal life, we have had some uneasiness about whether these positions falsify or debase the ideal role model which we have seen as essential to professional functioning. The foregoing analysis of authority relationships suggests a theoretical step which can open the way to more flexible examination of various kinds of practice. It may well be that the social worker-client relationship can occur within a variety of role designs which can be subsumed under a more highly generalized model. Within the basic definition of these reciprocal roles would be found a number of somewhat differently designed positions which take into account client need and the resulting distribution of decisions between worker and client.

We noted in our examination of an authority action in an institution that the design of the inmate role produced inherent but often un-observed strains in the inmate's relationship with authority, and that these strains could seriously interfere with the inmate's ability to work constructively with the authority person. It may well be that the prevailing role design for social worker-client relationships actually poses inherent and insuperable conflicts for individuals in certain social groups who need and could otherwise use our services.[1] If this is so it may be due to the fact that our current generalized role model includes decision-making patterns appropriate to certain social work positions but not to others, and that we need to formulate our ideal model at a higher level of generalization. This would open the way for profes-sional experimentation with role design where need is evident.

We have already made a number of steps in the direction of this kind of a formulation. The profession made a significant adjustment to client perception of the client position when fee service was provided in private agencies in order to make it possible for persons from higher income groups to use our services. And some of the techniques in use with hard-to-reach families and groups represent efforts to design the details of the client position so that persons with lower-class cultural patterns can participate in the social task for which the agency is

[1] See August B. Hollingshead and Frederick C. Redlich, *Social Class and Mental Illness* (John Wiley & Sons, Inc., New York, 1958), pp. 130-5, for a description of characteristic expectations of such groups.

organized. Empirical evidence would suggest that two areas of social work practice which call for re-examination of role design are found in corrections and institutional work.

3. *The decision-making team in the social services*

Our analysis suggests still a third area which invites exploration. We have noted that the authority relationship between the worker and his client is affected by the operation of the decision-making team which is active in relation to a given case. Who makes what decisions and how decisions are shared among the representatives of the different sanctioning systems set a determining framework for the ultimate decision process as it occurs between the worker and the client.

Examples of how these differently constituted teams affect the exercise of authority by the worker were elaborated in a seminar of thirty persons who represented several different fields of social service. According to those present in this seminar, a serious authority problem in public welfare occurs in relating the decisions of different categorical aids to the service needs of a particular client. For mental hygiene services, on the other hand, authority problems appeared particularly crucial in the relationships among the different professions. In child welfare, authority problems were identified at the point of integrating services from public and private agencies or from legal and service agencies for the same client. In corrections, a special problem appeared when the social worker shared responsibility for decisions with police and judges.

In each of these fields of service, problems in making constructive use of authority with the client seemed to be exacerbated by unresolved authority problems at the level of the team which is responsible for service decisions. As the examples given above were reported, it was evident that these problems were not simply matters of poor relationships among persons but were rooted deeply in communication and action difficulties deriving from the fact that each team member was responsible to a different sanctioning system with its own definition of values, goals, and appropriate methods of action. Such problems are inherent in complex decision-making. They are of such importance to effective service that they indicate the need for careful professional attention to the various patterns by which different service teams make shared decision-making effective in service to the client.

At the present level of development in social work theory it is no longer intellectually defensible to analyse the dynamics of authority for one field of service alone. A finding in one field that authority relationships are important in determining the nature of service leads us inevitably to ask: Does authority enter into all social worker-client relationships and, if so, in what ways? Since authority arises from the structural arrangements by which people are organized to do a job, it is probable that we will discover a range of patterns for authority relationships in the variously organized fields of service in which social workers are employed. A theoretical formulation about authority for the profession should include the concepts and principles which are common to use of authority by social workers wherever they work as well as the variables which determine differential adaptation of the generic theory within various fields of service. It is suggested that one way of making progress towards understanding authority as a dynamic in professional social work practice is to examine various kinds of social work practice in the framework of this analysis with special attention to problem areas.

GEORGE ALLEN & UNWIN LTD
Head Office:
40 Museum Street, London WC1
Telephone: 01-405 8577

Sales, Distribution and Accounts Departments:
Park Lane, Hemel Hempstead, Hertfordshire
Telephone: 0442 3244

Argentina: Defensa 681–5J, Buenos Aires
Australia: Cnr. Bridge Road and Jersey Street, Hornsby, N.S.W. 2077
Bangladesh: Empire Buildings, Victoria Park South, Dacca
Canada: 2330 Midland Avenue, Agincourt, Ontario
Greece: 3 Mitropoleous Street, Athens 118
India: 103/5 Walchand Hirachand Marg, Post Box 21, Bombay 1BR
285J Bepin Behari Ganguli Street, Calcutta 12
2/18 Mount Road, Madras 2
4/21–22B Asaf Ali Road, New Delhi 1
Japan: 29/13 Hongo 5 Chome, Bunkyo Ku, Tokyo 113
Kenya: P.O. Box 30583, Nairobi
Malaysia: 54 Jalan-Pudu, Room 303, Kuala Lumpur
New Zealand: 46 Lake Road, Northcote, Auckland 9
Nigeria: P.O. Box 62 Ibadan
Pakistan: Karachi Chambers, McLeod Road, Karachi 2
22 Falettis' Hotel, Egerton Road, Lahore
Philippines: U.P., P.O. Box 10, Quezon City, D-505
Singapore and Hong Kong: 53L Anson Road, 11th Floor Anson Centre, Singapore 2
South Africa: P.O. Box 31487, Braamfontein, Johannesburg
Thailand: P.O. Box 6/1, Bangkok
West Indies: Rockley New Road, St. Lawrence 4, Barbados